YOUR INTERNET CASH MACHINE

THE INSIDERS' GUIDE TO MAKING BIG MONEY, FAST!

Joe Vitale
Jillian Coleman Wheeler

WILEY

JOHN WILEY & SONS, INC.

Published by John Wiley & Sons, Inc., Hoboken, New Jersey.
Published simultaneously in Canada.

For general information on our other products and services or for technical support, please contact our Customer Care Department within the United States at (800) 762-2974, outside the United States at (317) 572-3993 or fax (317) 572-4002.

Wiley also publishes its books in a variety of electronic formats. Some content that appears in print may not be available in electronic books. For more information about Wiley products, visit our web site at www.wiley.com.

Library of Congress Cataloging-in-Publication Data:

Vitale, Joe, 1953–
    Your internet cash machine : the insiders guide to making big money, fast! / Joe Vitale, Jillian Coleman Wheeler.
      p. cm.
    ISBN 978-0-470-12944-9 (cloth)
      1. Electronic commerce. 2. Information technology.   3. Internet.
  I. Wheeler, Jillian Coleman, 1947– II. Title.
  HF5548.32.V58   2008
  658.8'72—dc22

                    2007024228

Printed in the United States of America.

10 9 8 7 6 5 4 3 2 1

This book is dedicated to
every aspiring entrepreneur in
search of his or her perfect business.
Welcome to the following pages!

CONTENTS

Acknowledgments   xiii

Foreword   xv

PART ONE   BUILDING THE FOUNDATION

It All Begins with You   **3**

Structure   3

Your Life and Your Business   4

What Is Your Current Situation?   5

What Are Your Interests, Talents, or Expertise?   7

What Are Your Desires?   8

Your Ideal Day   10

Guest Expert Article:
Creating Abundance In Your Career
(Thomas L. Pauley and Penelope J. Pauley)   11

Select the Best Business Model for You   **17**

Bring Your Off-Line Business Online   17

Guest Expert Article:
   Get Your Real Estate Business Online
   (Larry Goins)   21

Sales of Physical Products   23

Support Services for the World Wide Web   26

News and General Information Sites   26

Blogs   28

Entertainment Sites   31

Auction Sites   33

Affiliate Sales Sites   33

Social Networking Sites/Forums   34

Sale of Information Products   36

Education Sites   37

Guest Expert Article:
   Educating for Entrepreneurship
   (Rhea Perry)   38

Membership Sites   40

Multilevel Marketing/Network Marketing   40

Guest Expert Article:
   Geometric Giving: The Easy Way to Donate
   $1 Million a Month to Charity
   (Paulie Sabol)   43

Gambling and Adult Sites   46

A Closer Look at Online Auctions   50

Getting Started on eBay   51

What to Sell?   54

Pricing 56

Buying for Resale on Auction Sites 58

Promoting Your Auctions 60

Shipping 60

Timing Your Auction 61

The Path of the PowerSeller 62

Treat it like a Real Business 63

Bells and Whistles 64

How to Leverage eBay 64

Guest Expert Article:
  eBay and Beyond (Jim Cochrum) 65

A Closer Look at Affiliate Sales Sites 70

Advantages 70

Making Money as an Affiliate 71

How to Select Merchant Partners 72

Include Valuable Content 77

Google AdSense 78

Marketing through Social Networking Sites 80

Guest Expert Article:
  Use MySpace to Build Your eBay Business
  (Adam Ginsberg) 81

Guest Expert Article:
  A New Model of Social Networking
  (Sam Heyer) 83

Create Your Own Information Products   87

What Is an Information Product?   87

Determining Demand   88

Delivery   89

Benefits of Information Products   89

Guest Expert Article:
What's the Best Product to Sell Online?
Why, Information, of Course (Tim Knox)   90

Guest Expert Article:
How to Make and Sell a Video Product
at Zero Cost (Nerissa Oden)   95

PART TWO   THE ACTION STEPS

Set Up Your Web Site   105

Equip Yourself   105

Get Your Piece of Internet Real Estate   106

Guest Expert Article:
Profitably Naming Your New Internet Business
(Marcia Yudkin)   107

Find the Best Web Host   110

Set Up Your Infrastructure   111

Design Your Web Site   114

Physical Construction of Your Site   117

The Single-Page Sales Site   119

Guest Expert Article:
Three Secrets to Making Your Sales Letters Sell
(Mark Hendricks)   121

Get the Word Out   **127**

E-Mail Marketing   127

Articles   128

Search Engine Optimization   129

Your Blog   132

Branding   134

Joint Ventures   134

Your Affiliate Program   139

Newsletters   140

Newsgroups   140

Press Releases/Public Relations   140

Guest Expert Article:
Publicity Secrets to Attain Massive Success
for Your Internet Business (Annie Jennings)   141

Teleseminars and Webinars   145

Guest Expert Article:
Webinars—The Future of Online Marketing
(Jim Edwards)   145

Other Ways to Increase Traffic and Grow
Your List   147

Guest Expert Article:
Build Your List with Pay per Click
(Simon Leung)   150

Guest Expert Article:
Made You Look! (Wendi Friesen)   152

Make it Hypnotic!   **157**

What Is Hypnotic Writing?   158

The Formula for Causing Action   159

The Updated Formula   162

What about Your Web Site?   163

How Long Is Too Long?   166

How People Think   167

How to Create Hypnotic Stories   168

Reminders as Triggers   170

Guest Expert Article:
Buying Trances: The Real Secret to Hypnotic
Selling (Dr. Joe Vitale)   171

Changing Average Writing into Hypnotic Writing   176

Final Thoughts   181

PART THREE   GROW YOUR BUSINESS!

It's All About Quality   **185**

No Place to Hide   186

Deliver on Customer Service   186

Go Beyond Your Customer's Expectations   187

Guest Expert Article:
Make Sure Your Customers Actually Get
the Benefits (Bill Harris)   188

Build Your Business Support Network   194

The Power of the Mastermind Group   194

Guest Expert Article:
   Mastermind Groups for Internet Marketers
   (Bill Hibbler)   195

The Fine Art of Delegation   198

Comply with Cyber Law   200

Spam   200

Copyrights   201

Trademarks   201

Free Speech   202

Guest Expert Article:
   Legal Issues for Internet Marketers
   (Bob Silber)   202

Plan for Success   205

Your Business Plan   205

Incorporation   207

Guest Expert Article:
   How to Predict Your Way to Wealth
   (Mike Mograbi)   208

Index   217

ACKNOWLEDGMENTS

From Joe:

Thanks to Jillian for the book idea, and for all your hard work. Thank you, Nerissa (and the critters), for your love, patience, and support that make my writing time possible.

From Jillian:

Thanks to Joe and to Tom and Diane Pauley, for helping me get started in this wonderful business!

Thanks to my family: to Dempsey, for your constant love and support, and to my children and grandchildren for your patience in giving up some of our time together.

I particularly want to thank Cheryl Cromer, Genevieve Vaughan, and Jerry Minshew for your practical assistance when it was most needed, and the community of sisters and friends whose spirituality, love, and encouragement continually enrich my life.

FOREWORD

From Jew Central to Islam Online

Mark Joyner

As I write this Foreword, I just finished giving a talk in Singapore to 2,500 budding Internet entrepreneurs about how the world has already changed—and how some of us will wake up to this new reality and prosper while others will remain asleep and go the way of the dinosaur.

My friend Joe Vitale just sent me an e-mail from Wimberley, Texas, which I read in my Singapore hotel room. He asked if I'd write the Foreword to a new book he had just finished writing with Jillian Wheeler.

I met Jillian years ago at a seminar I hosted in Los Angeles, and Joe is an old-soul friend of mine whom I love deeply—not a fair-weather "I love him when he promotes my stuff" friend, but a true friend whose friendship transcends our differences and meets somewhere in that space where differences don't matter and all people are one. Hold that thought . . .

I said yes without even having read this book.

In this moment, I sit in the Singapore airport in a little jazz bar after a quick visit to the Philippines to see some close friends—on the way back to Auckland, New Zealand, where this former U.S. Army officer and eternal lover of America now resides.

I just demonstrated to you how this new world works. I demonstrated a new sensibility. Did you catch it? If not, here are a few more clues.

You may notice that my decision to write this review was based on real human connections, not on some cold sense of what I think will be profitable.

You'll also notice that location was simply not an issue.

These connections have already transcended space and time because of the way e-mail detaches us from location and time. Joe can write the e-mail in Texas on Thursday and I can read it in Singapore on Saturday and it just doesn't matter.

Are you catching it yet? Well, there's a bit more than meets the eye.

Joe understood, I'm sure, without me even saying it, that my yes was conditional. Joe knows that my yes would be totally dependent on my looking at the book and liking it.

Fifty years ago this would likely have not been the case. Back then, things that sucked could be promoted to the gills and would still be successful purely on the merits of the hype.

This is true today, but the life cycle of things that suck is much shorter than it would have been 50 years ago—even if the arc of that life cycle is steeper today. You see, that which sucks today can rise quickly if hyped intensely, but it will come down crashing just as quickly because of its suckiness.

Not so 50 years ago. *Suck* could be masked by hype back then. Ownership of communication media would allow hypesters to drown out truth with a loud, singular voice. Today, the ownership of communication (along with the ownership of other forms of power) is decentralizing.

This is why you can see a reference to the web sites Jew Central and Islam Online on the same page of the book you are about to read, and no one will bat an eye.

I believe that people love the same things—and each other—despite the surface differences. This truth is being proven again and again as we watch the new dynamics brought on by the Internet unfold.

So what does any of this have to do with a book about doing business on the Internet? Well, it's sort of a skeleton key that unlocks every important door of e-commerce success. I'll spell it out for you, if you haven't figured it out yet:

1. Treat people with respect.
2. Make products that don't suck.

If you don't understand why these are the new rules of the road, go ahead and try operating under the old rules for a while—(1) you over everyone else and (2) hype over quality—and I'm sure your skinned knees will put you on the right track.

I'm not too worried, though. Knee-skinning happens fast these days.

PART ONE

Building the Foundation

IT ALL BEGINS WITH YOU

I n this book, we tell everything you need to know about doing
business on the Internet. We guide you as you select a business
model, and we give you a clear, powerful plan with action steps
you can follow. We lead you to the tools that will make your
work easier and more profitable.

STRUCTURE

The information we are sharing with you has been organized into three
sections. Part One guides you through planning and building the foundation of your Internet Cash Machine. Part Two shows you the action
steps, and Part Three gives you tools to grow your business over
time. Each section is important, and we encourage you to read them
in order.

Throughout the book, you'll find "Guest Expert" articles. We have
asked a few of our friends, each an expert in his or her field, to contribute specialized knowledge we think will be invaluable to you. At
the end of each chapter, you will find a Resource Page with extra help
and links to Internet sites. Be sure and read these Resource Pages.

Please note: URLs change frequently, and by the time you read
this book, some of the web site addresses we have cited may have
changed. We suggest you enter the name of the site into a search
engine such as Google to find the most current URLs.

YOUR LIFE AND YOUR BUSINESS

A new business doesn't grow in a vacuum. It grows in the context of your life. So before we get into the nuts and bolts of the book, we would like to spend a few moments telling you about our philosophy of business and life. We also share with you some processes we think you'll find very helpful.

First, we're excited about the world of Internet business. We believe we are poised at the very beginning of a new world economy. The basis of our economic system is moving away from the soulless, impersonal corporation, and toward businesses owned and operated by individuals and small groups of people. Small business has always been important in every country of the world, of course, but with the advent of the World Wide Web, individual businesses are now in a position to create significant wealth with minimal infrastructure and a manageable amount of investment and effort. This trend will only continue to grow and expand. You can be part of it.

We believe there are no accidents. Everything that happens in life is purposeful. Every event and every experience offers us the opportunity to learn and grow, and to move forward toward the life we desire. Even the most challenging, most painful experiences can be transformed, like lead into gold, to create beauty.

We have both lived through difficult times. Joe was homeless for a while. Jillian was a single mom who, for a few months, survived on food stamps. We have lost jobs. We've each been through a divorce. People we loved have died. We have overcome depression and hopelessness.

Today we are both well known, with very successful businesses. We have beautiful homes and loving relationships. We used a number of mental and spiritual tools to reach this point, and describing them all is not the purpose of this book. Briefly, we each created a clear mental picture of the life we wanted, and we held a firm intention to have that life. Each step of the way, as much as humanly possible, we remained conscious of and grateful for every good thing in our lives. We refused to spend time focusing on what we did not have, and we kept our attention and our imaginations fixed on our visions of our ideal lives—the direction in which we firmly believed we were heading. We were patient and we were totally committed. We took action as we were inspired, and every day we moved more fully into the amazing realities we are living today.

We respect your personal belief system, whether or not you are religious or spiritual. We believe there is a guiding intelligence in the Universe. That guiding intelligence has a plan for each of us, a way in which we can each contribute to the world in which we live. The key to figuring out your personal plan is to pay attention to your desires. If there is a desire in your heart, and that desire is inherently good (that is, it does no harm to you or to any other person), then pay attention! Act on your desires, and watch your plan unfold.

We each have a desire to write, to teach, and to run our own businesses. We happen to like keeping business simple. Some of our friends in the world of Internet marketing have created large, complex businesses with many employees. A few even own office buildings. We think that's fine for them, but it isn't for us.

We each have a desire to work at home, close to the people we love and close to our creature comforts. We like taking a break and slipping into the pool or, in Joe's case, going out to his backyard gym to work out. We like taking naps in the middle of the day. We like going out to meet friends for coffee if we get the urge. We believe in giving back, and we both do that in various ways.

We like traveling to interesting places. Joe loves to relax in Hawaii. On a recent speaking trip, he fell in love with Poland. Jillian and her family spend a lot of time in the Pacific Northwest and in Mexico. When their younger children are all comfortably settled in college, she and her husband plan to live in Europe for a couple of years. After all, we can run our Internet businesses from anywhere in the world. All we need is a high-speed Internet connection.

We are definitely entrepreneurs. We think it is likely you are an entrepreneur, also, or you would not be reading this book. Entrepreneurs are a unique kind of human being. We speak a different language than other people, because we see greater possibilities. We wrote this book so we could speak that language to you, and you could take what we have learned and live your plan—the life you desire.

WHAT IS YOUR CURRENT SITUATION?

When you begin a new venture, you don't have to know in advance every step you are going to take. As a matter of course, each phase you enter on your journey will present you with new choices. But you do need to have an idea for the first few steps. So let's begin there. As you go through this section (and every other section of this book), we recommend you keep a notebook nearby and write down your thoughts and ideas.

Where are you now in terms of your work situation? Are you employed in a job you like, or at least find tolerable? If so, you may be thinking of starting your Internet business on a part-time basis. That is absolutely viable. Many profitable Internet businesses are operated part-time by people who work at real jobs. Many more began as part-time businesses and grew to full time.

Are you a housewife, a college student, or a disabled person interested in supplementing your existing income? An Internet business is a great way to bring more money into your household. In fact, many women have begun small Internet businesses that have grown to the point that their husbands have left other jobs to join the business, and the kids are working there, too. Many college students have built incomes that exceed the amount they would otherwise eventually earn using their degrees.

We have a friend who was a musician when he was diagnosed with multiple sclerosis. Faced with the decline of his physical capabilities and his ability to play music, he and his wife started an Internet business that continues to provide for all their needs. You can read about him at www.ClayCotton.com, or visit his long-term care insurance site at www.prepsmart.com.

Have you recently left a job or been laid off? That is how Jillian got into Internet marketing. She was doing marketing for a software company, bringing in a high salary at a terrific job she loved. Then the software industry crashed, and she, along with thousands of other people, was suddenly unemployed. For two years, she looked for marketing jobs, but when companies are not making money, they slash their marketing budgets. She had been a grants, business, and government relations consultant for many years before that, but she really didn't want to go out soliciting new clients. It felt like going backward.

Throughout those two years, her friends Tom and Diane Pauley were growing their Internet business, and they kept encouraging her to give it a try. Tom introduced Jillian to Joe Vitale, who was a neighbor, and Joe was encouraging as well. Eventually, she stepped into the unknown. She set up a web site to train people how to find and write grants and establish nonprofit organizations. From the first year, her business made good money.

Jillian's husband was employed during this period (today he, too, works in their businesses), so her family had a reliable source of support. We do not recommend you leave a job cold turkey to start an Internet business, unless you have savings or some other income. But if you are already jobless, that may give you the incentive you need to work hard and smart and fast to get your business off the ground. You can do it. We personally know hundreds of people, and we know of many more thousands, who have created wealthy lives for themselves and their families, through their Internet businesses.

WHAT ARE YOUR INTERESTS, TALENTS, OR EXPERTISE?

We firmly believe business should be fun. Life is simply too short not to have fun all the time. Also, fun will help you get through the times when you must work long hours, as you may in the beginning or when you have a big project.

Your heart wants to have fun. If you are doing work you dislike, you will find a way to unconsciously sabotage it. Loving your work and having fun working take you a long way toward success in your business.

What is fun for you? If you love riding motorcycles, you may build an Internet business about bikes. If you love golf, or tennis, or sailing, you may choose to build your business around your sport.

Do you knit, do needlepoint, or crochet? Do you make your own clothes? Then your craft may lead to your chosen business. Are you an artist? A musician? A filmmaker? Your Internet business may involve your art.

How have you made a living thus far? If you are a dentist, an architect, a carpet cleaner, a plumber, or a word processor, you have skills that can form the basis of your new business. In fact, tens of thousands of workers—professional, technical, blue collar, and clerical—have already translated their experience and skills into profitable Internet businesses.

Are you a mother or father? If you are successfully parenting your children, you have one of the most important life skills in the world. Are you a good cook? Have you learned how to maintain a happy and rewarding relationship with your spouse? You have information to share, and a potential business niche.

Absolutely any interest, talent, or skill can form the basis of a successful Internet business, provided there are enough other people on the World Wide Web who are looking for what you have to offer. In other words, is there a market for your business? In this book we show you how to find the answer to that question.

WHAT ARE YOUR DESIRES?

If you are like most people, you have probably spent a lot of your life living the way other people wanted you to live. When you were young, your parents made the rules. They decided the location of your home, which school you would attend, and what time you would get up and go to bed. If they were particularly enlightened, they may have encouraged you to find your own passion and follow it. But if they were like many loving yet clueless parents, they may have told you what sports to play and what music lessons to take.

Later on, your lover or spouse, or your friends, may have set up the parameters of your life. If you live with someone who hates the outdoors, it may be easier to give up your desire to fish and camp than to argue about how to spend your time. If you have a secret desire to play the flute, but your friends would think you were weird, you may have decided to keep that desire under wraps. Little by little, that is how we give up our joy.

Your single biggest obstacle to living the life you desire may be your job. Your boss probably expects you to get to work at a specific time. You may be trapped inside an office eight hours a day. You may have little contact with other people, or more contact than is comfortable for you. Worst of all, you may be bored, never challenged to give the gifts you have to offer the world.

If you were to live exactly as you desire, how would that look?

Here are some questions you can ask yourself, to help answer that question. Feel free to write the answers here in the book.

Process 1

> What time do I like to get up in the morning?
> What time do I like to go to bed?
> At what hour do I want to begin working? When am I most
> productive?

When is my energy highest?

What do I want to spend the majority of my time doing? Here are some possible answers:

- Write
- Engage in technical work, such as programming or building web sites
- Plan
- Organize
- Design graphics
- Conceptualize products
- Create something with my hands
- Make movies
- Make music
- Teach
- Speak
- Mentor other.

Do I want to work at home?

Do I want to go out to an office?

How much time do I want to spend inside?

How much time do I want to spend outside in the world?

What type of physical surroundings do I desire?

Do I want a window out into nature? What type of view do I desire? Or would I prefer an inside space, to help me concentrate?

What physical activity do I want to incorporate into my day? When?

How much time do I want to spend with other people?

How much time do I want to spend alone?

Do I want to work alone, or do I want a partner or associates?

Do I want to manage other people? Have employees? Or work on my own, and contract with others when I need assistance?

How much time do I want to spend with family and friends?

What activities would I like to do with them?

Do I want to travel? How much?

What hobbies do I want to do?

Do I want to engage in continuing education? What type?

There are undoubtedly other questions you can think of for yourself.

Process 2

Here is another process you may have done in the past. It is powerful, and we suggest you do it at least every year. Ask yourself:

> If I knew I had only one year to live, how would I spend my time?
> How would I change my relationships?
> What would I want to leave behind?

Of course, it is wise for us to work now for our future well-being and the well-being of our families. The ability to delay gratification is one of the markers of maturity. However, life comes with no guarantees as to the length of time we will be on the planet. We believe in balancing the work we do to build our futures with living fully and joyously in each present moment.

YOUR IDEAL DAY

Process 3

Here is another, very powerful process. Take some time when you are completely alone, and will not be interrupted. Sit quietly in a comfortable chair, and close your eyes. Imagine you are living an ideal day. Begin by imagining waking up in the morning, feeling very comfortable in your body. As you open your eyes, are you alone or with your partner? Do you spend the first few moments cuddling, maybe talking over your plans for the day?

Or do you get right up on your own, perhaps make a cup of tea, and go sit on your patio? Perhaps you do some yoga, or meditate. Maybe you go for an early walk, or go to the gym. What would you like for breakfast?

If you have children at home, your mornings may be quite different. Your day may begin when your little ones climb into your bed and wake you up. Or you may need to go awaken older children, prepare their breakfast, and help them start their day. In that case, you may visualize those activities proceeding peacefully, with everyone in the family being cooperative and calm and loving.

Every state of life has its own joys and challenges. You may be married or single, childless or with children, in your twenties, thirties, or any decade beyond. You may be a member of a religious order. The point of this process is to imagine a day in this life you have chosen, unfolding in the way you see as ideal.

Continue to visualize your entire day, on through until you go to bed. Take plenty of time imagining the portion of your day devoted to work. Then, when you have fully visualized your day, write it down. Write the story of your ideal day, from that first moment you open your eyes until the moment you fall asleep.

This exercise may take several days to complete. Most people are so busy coping with the challenges of each day, they seldom step back and imagine how it *could* be if they had their ideal day. You may find it quite difficult to think of what you want. But until you let yourself get in touch with what you truly desire, and hold a picture of those desires, you will not achieve them. As soon as you complete this process, you will be astonished how quickly your life will begin to transform in wonderful ways.

Our first guest expert article is by Tom and Penelope Pauley. They have made millions in their own Internet businesses, and they specialize in teaching others how to live rich lives.

GUEST EXPERT ARTICLE

CREATING ABUNDANCE IN YOUR CAREER

Thomas L. Pauley and Penelope J. Pauley

You were born rich. Whether you know it or not, whether you recognize it or not, whether you allow it or not, you were born rich. Regardless of the condition of your checkbook or what you think is true in your life, you were born rich. Because at birth you were given a great and awesome power.

You were given the power to draw to you absolutely anything you desire. You can have anything you want in this life. You can live the life you know in your heart is yours to live. In fact, you

---

(Continued)

were meant to have that life. And all you have to do is ask and allow yourself to receive. That's the gift that will bring abundance into your life and your business. What's more, it's a natural law—a universal law. And it's as old as creation.

You have the power to get what you want by simply asking for it.

Take this book you're reading, for example. You were drawn to this book. You've been asking for more money and success in your life, and that desire has attracted you to this book. This book gives you the physical tools you need to get started in a relatively technical business. It's an education in how to do the mundane things necessary to create a vehicle for your money to find you. But the business you create is never going to be the source of your success. It's just a vehicle. The real source of your wealth is your amazing power to attract anything you want in life.

Now you may find this part shocking. The reason you are not rolling in cash today is because you *don't really want* more money in your life. And this is your biggest obstacle to success in any business.

Oh, I know you *think* you want more cash. You probably make a fuss about not having enough all the time. Obviously you want more. Every time you see the bills or that car you'd love to have, but can't afford; every time you think about all the things that don't fit into your budget—the new furniture, the new clothes, dinner out at a fine restaurant . . . You want it all. So, saying that you don't want an abundance of cash in your life is ridiculous, right?

Wrong.

Every time you make a negative comment, every time you say you can't or won't or shouldn't, you're telling the Universe no.

"I can't afford that car." "I'll have to wait on those new shoes." "I just don't have enough money for a nice dinner!" "Money's tight." "I have a lot of expenses this month." "Instead of having money left at the end of the month, there's always 'month' left at the end of the 'money.'" "Look at that guy—I'll bet his parents bought that car."

Every time you bad-mouth money, you're saying "I don't want any."

All of these negative expressions are orders. You are telling the Universe exactly what to do: "Keep the money tight." "Don't let me afford that car." "I want to wait on the new shoes."

You can read all the books in creation. You can start a million businesses, but unless you clean up your asking, you'll just keep getting more of what you've already gotten so far.

You must talk, think, and write in positives.

"That's my car, that Mercedes Benz GL450." "I'm going to Paris this year." "I have a great new outfit for that special dinner." "I'm going to have a great month financially." "I have more income than I can spend." Ask for what you want as though you already have it. That tells the universe that you are serious.

Positive requests bring positive results. We talk about this in great detail in the book my daughter and I wrote, *I'm Rich Beyond My Wildest Dreams—I am. I am. I am.* It's the story of how we created a rich and happy life practically overnight and the system we used to get there.

We suggest you ask for what you want in the present tense using simple written parameters. "I have my new Mercedes. It is Everest green. It is easily paid for." Never the future tense. Never write, "I will have my new Mercedes," because you don't want it in the future. Tomorrow never comes. You want that car *now*. You want to drive it now. Love it now. Don't ask to want something, or you'll forever want it.

Of course, asking is only half the equation. You must also allow yourself to receive, which is the hardest part of all. We are all caught up with doubts and fears about our own value, or about whether we've worked hard enough and long enough to justify having what we really want. "Put your nose to the grindstone." "The harder I work the luckier I get." "It's the early bird that gets the worm."

Come on! All birds get worms. Nobody in his right mind will put his nose on a grindstone. I'm Irish, so don't even get me started about luck. Luck is simply receiving without putting up a fight.

This work and slave nonsense has been hammered into our brains since we were old enough to watch TV. You get it in school. You get it from your parents. You get it everywhere.

Why do you think people like Donald Trump, Bill Gates, and Mark Cuban have so much money? Do you really think it's because they worked their backsides off 18 hours a day and saved religiously? Give me a break! They got rich because they allowed it. They

(Continued)

asked for outrageous success and then they allowed themselves to receive it.

Working long, hard hours is not the secret to success.

Oh, you may work some long, hard hours building your Internet cash machine. But that's not the secret to your success. The secret is allowing yourself to be rich. The secret is having a dream, asking for that dream to become a reality, and then allowing it to reach you.

When we started our online business we worked long, hard hours for two years. Because we loved it! It was a joy to create something of our own. I'd worked my whole life making other people rich and the only thing I had to show for it was two personal bankruptcies and the opportunity to start from scratch in a rented two-bedroom condo when I should have been planning retirement cruises.

I asked for my Internet success and I allowed myself to receive it. Building it was the best part. What a ride! It was like living a dream. We still tell stories of those times. We were doing what we loved, and watching our success unfold every day was priceless.

Now I make more money some days than most people make in a year. And you can be absolutely sure of one thing: Those 14-hour days are not on my to-do list anymore.

You can do this.

You can have absolutely anything you want in life. All you have to do is ask and allow yourself to receive. Now here's a secret to facilitate your receiving: No matter what happens, no matter how tight the cash flow seems or how difficult the learning curve, keep your dreams on the front burner. Focus not on what you think life is giving you. Focus only on how you want your life to be. Think only of your dreams. Don't ignore problems, either; just know the Universe can change anything instantly.

Then nothing can ever stop you or your abundance. Because in truth there is only one person is this entire world who can stop you from succeeding. There is only one person who can destroy your Internet cash machine. You know who it is. You see him or her every morning when you look in the mirror.

Now, this is a short chapter and we don't have time to give you all the tools we used for getting rich. But we can give you seven free lessons and an hour-long audio called *The Three Keys to Success*. Go to RichDreams.com and join the Rich Dreams News. That newsletter alone has empowered so many just like you to reach and enjoy the life of which you dream.

Ask. Allow. Focus on what you want—and *only* on what you want. Ignore the naysayer. Stay the course. That's the secret to building a magnificent life and a powerful Internet cash machine.

Let us know about your success and that new car. You were born rich, remember? Creating an Internet cash machine should be a piece of cake. You have all the resources of the entire universe at your command after all. Good luck and great adventures.

Tom Pauley and Penelope Pauley, father/daughter authors, of I'm Rich Beyond My Wildest Dreams—I am. I am. I am.*, provide courses, e-books, MP3s, and CDs that can help you create abundance in your life. Their transforming programs, "Quantum Marketing" and "Quantum Selling," are revolutionizing personal and business development worldwide. Join their free newsletter at www.richdreams.com and get seven free lessons and an hour-long MP3 detailing the Three Keys to Success.*

Resource Page

Summary of topics discussed in this chapter:
- ☛ There are three sections in this book:
    - ☛ Part One: "It All Begins with You."
    - ☛ Part Two: "The Action Steps."
    - ☛ Part Three: "Grow Your Business."
- ☛ Your business grows in the context of your life.
- ☛ Assess your current situation.
- ☛ Inventory your interests, talents, and expertise.
- ☛ Write down your desires.
- ☛ Describe your ideal day.

Guest experts Tom and Penelope Pauley write about how to create abundance in your career.

Go to www.YourInternetCashMachine.com and access much more free information, including additional questionnaires to help you identify your interests and desires for your life and your business. Enjoy interviews with our guest experts. Claim your free membership now!

SELECT THE BEST BUSINESS MODEL FOR YOU

You have made a crucial decision in your life, to move forward with an Internet business. Congratulations! Now it's time to choose your business model. Where will you focus your efforts and your energy?

Following is a discussion of the most popular Internet business models. Most of them can be initiated with a small investment, while some require a more complex infrastructure. We recommend you read them all and notice what ideas come to you. Then select one model to get started. Concentrate on building your business from that model. Later, you may decide to expand and incorporate other models.

BRING YOUR OFF-LINE BUSINESS ONLINE

If you own a business with a physical storefront, an office where you meet clients or treat patients, or a gallery where you hang paintings, you are doing business in the off-line world. In online-world jargon, you have a *bricks-and-mortar* business. Do you also have an Internet presence? If not, it's time you move to the next level: *bricks and clicks*.

There are compelling reasons to create an Internet presence for your business, or more fully develop your existing site. The first, very basic reason is visibility. Sixty-four percent of U.S. households now have Internet access, and 31 percent of those who do not pay for Internet service at home have access at work. As Internet proficiency increases, fewer of your potential customers are reaching for their local yellow pages. Instead, they go online and use a search engine. Even if they are simply ordering a pizza, more and more hungry shoppers are turning to Google rather than a paper directory. We are not suggesting you discontinue your yellow pages listing, of course. Good marketing requires reaching out to customers through multiple channels. One distinct advantage of a web site over a paper ad, however, is your ability to make real-time, day-to-day changes in the content of your site.

Second, more and more of your potential customers are doing research online. For example, someone in the market for a tent used to trek all over town to sporting goods stores, comparing brands, features, and prices. Now, that same customer is more likely to find the information he needs online. Eighty-eight percent of people who sometimes shop online do product research on the Internet.

Third, your customers and your potential customers are definitely buying online. Studies show that 85 percent of adults with Internet access have made purchases online. Among households with an annual income above $75,000, that number jumps to a whopping 97 percent. ComScore Networks, a global Internet information provider, estimates $100 billion was spent online in 2006, exclusive of travel-related purchases.

Some forecasters believe the economy is poised on the cutting edge of a trend, in some market niches, completely away from brick-and-mortar businesses. Some businesses have already moved entirely to the Internet, while others have gone out of business perhaps to some degree as a result of online competition. It is too soon to know how business will change as we move forward in the Internet age. Clearly, however, the savvy business owner will get ahead of the curve.

In a nationwide survey of 53 small-business owners, whose annual sales ranged from less than $250,000 to over $5,000,000, 57 percent reported they have web sites. The survey revealed that a high percentage of this 57 percent believe their Internet site has improved the economic health of their business. Among the benefits they cited were greater resilience during economic downturns and a significant increase in the number of sales leads.

Of course, web sites operated by real-world businesses are not all the same. They run the gamut from one-page sites that are not much more than business cards, to fully performing commercial sites. Let's examine what may be right for your business.

If you are going to invest the money to build a web site and budget a monthly payment to have it hosted on a server, the very least you need is a site that functions as an attractive and informational brochure for your business. Like a paper brochure, your web site should describe your business and explain what products and services you provide. It must include your telephone number and fax number, your e-mail address (provided you are available to respond to inquiries), the location(s) of your business, and directions to get there.

Visitors to your web site might also enjoy learning about the history of your company, as well as your values and principles. If you have won awards or achieved particular distinction in your field, by all means include that. For example, if your restaurant was voted as serving "Best Greek Food" in your city, you will want to display that honor in a prominent place on the site. Also include any certifications or licenses held by the business or the business owners. Advertising specials and coupons are a good way to entice customers to choose your business over others.

Although more and more customers are buying online, only about 5 percent of online activity is related to making purchases. Most Internet activity is centered on a search for information. The smart business owner focuses on creating a relationship with visitors to his or her site, and building trust. A great way to do that is by providing valuable information.

For example, if you own a restaurant, you can provide articles about the history of a specific cuisine, and interesting tidbits and photographs about the part of the world where your cuisine originated. You might offer recipes. Customers enjoy visiting restaurants with a history, and seeing the old photographs they display on the wall. If your restaurant, or the building you occupy, or the part of town where you are located, is historic, put those photos on your web site.

If you sell shoes, tell people how to select the best footwear for them. Provide articles about foot health. Or, if your focus is high fashion, offer articles about the latest trends and styles. If you sell sports shoes, include sports articles. If you are a dentist, provide tips on how to maintain healthy gums. Make it fun and interesting to visit your site.

Imbue your web site with the culture of your business. If your culture is warm, welcoming, and personal, make sure your web site reflects that. If your culture is focused on performance and efficiency, emphasize those values on your site.

The big move, of course, will happen when you take your business to a full commercial web site—when you begin to sell online. Many businesses are natural candidates for online sales. You may already sell products in your bricks-and-mortar establishment that customers are eager to buy online. Even if your products do not seem like a fit for Internet commerce, keep an open mind. Many restaurants are selling their own lines of packaged food products, such as signature sauces. Movie theaters can sell tickets online, or movie posters. Hair salons can sell hair-styling products. Opticians can sell e-books on eye health. Consultants can sell their services, as we do.

One of the things that, for many businesses, stands in the way of creating an Internet presence is a sense of overwhelm. There is so much to learn, and business owners tend to be the kind of people who want to do it right and avoid mistakes. Consequently, they are slow to act. Business owners may want to go online, but they want their web sites to be perfect from the beginning.

We encourage you to let go of your reservations. The Internet is not a static medium. It is constantly changing, and individual web sites change as well. Instead of waiting until the perfect time, when you can create the perfect web site, just make the commitment to move forward with a simple site. Begin with the brochure site we mentioned earlier. Add information. Then, when you are ready, offer some products.

Although a web site is a natural extension of your off-line business, it is very important to understand that online business operates by a completely different set of rules and conventions. It is critical that you gain the skills to make your online business a success. We are here to show you how. Most of the advice we offer in the nuts-and-bolts sections of this book will be directly applicable to your bricks-and-mortar business.

Our second guest expert article, by Larry Goins, explains how one real estate investor took his off-line business online, with hugely profitable results.

GUEST EXPERT ARTICLE

GET YOUR REAL ESTATE BUSINESS ONLINE

Larry Goins

As I travel all over the country teaching real estate investors how to automate their business, one of the questions I get asked the most is, "How do I get my real estate business online like yours?" Well, that's a great question, and one that can easily be answered. But let's think about this for a minute. What exactly do we mean by getting your real estate business online? Well, you can have a web site, which seems like the most logical way, but there are many ways to get your off-line real estate business online.

In fact, you can have an extremely successful real estate business, operating it by phone, fax, FedEx, e-mail and Internet, and never have a web site at all. After all, that's how we buy and sell all of our properties. We didn't even have a web site until last year. I know it can be scary, thinking about buying and selling houses online, but it can be a very simple transition. In fact, when I created my system called the "Ultimate Buying and Selling Machine!" I made a commitment that I would not include any process or procedure that required any skills more technical than being able to send or receive an e-mail.

So what is the easiest and fastest way to start getting your real estate business online? Let's look at locating deals online first. There are many web sites to help you find deals online, and I want to give you some of the best categories to get started. But first, I want to help you get your online search system set up to maximize your time spent online.

There is a Web browser called Firefox that you can download free by going to www.mozilla.com. The Firefox browser has a lot of features that you will not find in most other browsers. One of the most useful is a feature called *tabbed browsing*. In most browsers, if you have a web site open and want to open another one but keep the first one open as well, you have to open up a whole new browser window. That wastes time and computer resources. With Firefox,

(Continued)

you simply click on a little button to open another tab within the existing window. The best part is you can open as many tabs to view as many web sites as you want within that one window. You can save entire groups of tabs as well. Let me give you an example.

In my market of real estate there are 11 different newspapers whose real estate classifieds we like to read. I started a group of tabs called "My Newspapers." I opened my Firefox browser and went to the first newspaper, the *Charlotte Observer*, clicked on "Classifieds" and then clicked on "Real estate." Once I found all of the listings, I bookmarked it in the "My Newspapers" group. Then I opened another tab, went to the next paper, clicked on "Classifieds," then on "Real estate," and when I found the listings I bookmarked that page. I continued to do this until I had all 11 newspapers open to the real estate listings of the classifieds, all in one window.

Now on Monday mornings, when we want to search for the newspaper listings, we simply open Firefox and open the group called "My Newspapers." It immediately opens and loads 11 different newspaper listings of real estate ads. We can search them in less than 15 minutes. Is that using technology or what? And the best part is, I haven't purchased a single newspaper yet.

In fact, if you like that, wait until you see what I did with this technology. After about 10 months of research I created a ready-made set of importable bookmarks you can import into your Firefox browser, and you can create a customized search like this for not only newspapers but real estate auctions, government auctions, for-sale-by-owner sites, realtor sites, bank-owned (REO) property sites, appraisal sites, county records sites, and much more. This tool is available in my course called the "Ultimate Buying and Selling Machine!"

Now that you have learned to locate properties on the Internet, you must be able to follow up with all of the prospects. You do this by creating a database of all of your contacts with autoresponders for weekly follow-up. You actually need four different types of contacts in your database. You need realtors, investors, for sale by owners, and you need retail buyers. You want to create specific autoresponders for each of these groups so that you are contacting them every week. I don't know of anyone in real estate, other than my employees or students, who contacts every person in their database every week, do you?

In fact, this is so important that I have created 12 months of autoresponder text for my students, so the work is already done for you. For example, every time we put a realtor in our database, they start getting an e-mail every week. Each e-mail refers to the previous time we spoke with them or the last e-mail we sent, and it always asks them for any properties they have on which we should make an offer. Our autoresponder e-mails also ask them for referrals of any rehab contractors, appraisers, attorneys, and lenders that they would recommend we do business with. After all, who knows who to use on your team better than the realtor, right?

These are just two of the many ways we automate our business and are doing business online, and that's even without a web site. I hope this has helped you see a few of the many options you can use not only in real estate but in any business.

I want to thank Jillian and Joe for allowing me to share some of our techniques for automating our real estate business online.

Visit www.LarryGoins.com and subscribe to Larry's free weekly newsletter. You can also listen to weekly training teleconferences, and learn how Larry buys and sells ten to fifteen houses a month and never looks at them, having them sold in less than two hours using his "Ultimate Buying and Selling Machine!" course. You will also receive two free e-books titled Twelve Deadly Mistakes Investors Make and How to Avoid Them *and* Think and Grow Rich, *plus lots of free forms and documents you can use in your real estate business.*

SALES OF PHYSICAL PRODUCTS

The buying and selling of merchandise has probably been around almost as long as humanity. It is likely the earliest humans traded with each other for the things they needed. About 10,000 years ago, our nomadic ancestors began to settle down and build towns. They erected shops and sold goods. For 9,995 of those 10,000 years, selling products meant having a physical location and a storefront from which to sell.

Today, it is a whole new world. Today you can open a retail business on the Internet. Having a physical store is optional, and often not even desirable. Let's compare the two paths.

When you open a retail store in the bricks-and-mortar world, you must choose a location. You will want to select a site that is easily found by potential customers, amidst a natural flow of traffic. When you find that location, you immediately limit your customer base to people willing to travel to your store.

Chances are you will lease the building you select, at least at first. Later, you may buy or build a structure you own. The better your location, the higher cost you will pay per square foot of space you occupy. After you select the location, you may be required to finish out the space. At the least, you will have to decorate and furnish your store. You will have to buy enough inventory to fill the store, and to restock the items you sell from the shelves.

In the beginning, you may be the only employee of your business. Perhaps you will enlist the participation of a spouse or friend. But as your business becomes successful, you will have to take on the role of boss. You will have to hire people and manage them. You will be responsible for payroll and benefits and the attendant taxes.

You will need to advertise, to let potential customers know you have opened for business. Advertising space in newspapers, local magazines, and radio is costly. You will spend several hundred dollars a year on yellow pages advertising alone. Starting and operating an offline business will cost tens of thousands of dollars, at least—money you must spend before you ever make a dime.

Now consider the online store. Your location will consist of the web site name (URL) you purchase. From that location on the World Wide Web, customers from every neighborhood, every city and country throughout the world, can come into your store and buy. You do not have to buy any furnishings or inventory. You can arrange with your suppliers to ship the merchandise you sell directly from their warehouse to the customer's door.

Your start-up costs can be a few hundred dollars. Your monthly operating costs will usually be less than $200, even with a highly sophisticated shopping cart, merchant account, and autoresponders. In an online business, your staffing needs will be greatly reduced. You may at some point hire employees, or contract out some services, but you will not need clerks standing behind a counter.

Remember the figures we quoted earlier: Five percent of time spent online by the average consumer is spent buying; the remaining

95 percent is spent gathering information. A great example of an online store that serves customers with information, as well as selling them products, is SixWise (http://www.sixwise.com). SixWise offers a variety of products of use to families. However, knowing that 95 percent of all web site visits do not result in a sale, SixWise concentrates on building relationships with potential customers over time by featuring articles of interest to families.

Although we refer in this section to freestanding web site stores, there are two good options for online sales of physical products that utilize existing platforms. The first is Yahoo! Stores. The second is eBay Stores.

It has been estimated that one of every eight stores on the Internet is hosted by Yahoo! Stores. Yahoo! offers three levels of stores. As of this writing, the Starter Store costs $39.95 per month (there are often special introductory prices at all levels of store), and a transaction fee of 1.5 percent per item. The Standard Store costs $99.95 per month, and a transaction fee of 1 percent per item. The Professional Store costs $299.95 per month, and a transaction fee of 0.75 percent per item. Both the Standard and the Professional Store options provide a variety of helpful features, such as gift certificates, coupons, and a cross-selling tool that suggests related purchases to customers as they buy. Real-time integration with back-end systems provides notification of availability of products in inventory as the customer checks out, and you can be apprised of new orders by fax when you are not online. Orders can automatically be exported to UPS for shipping, and the "Click Trails" and "Frequent Search Topics" reports enable you to analyze your customers' shopping patterns.

Later in this book we focus on the auction sites, including, of course, eBay. But eBay is more than just auctions. Many businesses, large and small, have established an eBay store from which to sell their products.

In order to open an eBay store, you must be a registered eBay seller, and you must have a feedback score of no less than 20. Three levels of stores are available. The Basic Store costs $15.95 per month. The Featured Store is $49.95 per month; it provides more advanced customization and tools and is geared for small companies that want to grow. An Anchor Store costs $499.95 per month, and provides marketing benefits such as 24-hour live telephone support from eBay staff.

The Anchor Store is for high-volume sellers who intend to move a significant amount of merchandise.

In addition to the monthly fee, eBay store owners incur an additional small fee for each product listed and sold, and if you utilize PayPal, you will also pay them a fee. All three levels of eBay stores provide you with complimentary listing and selling tools, including Turbo Lister, which facilitates importing inventory data.

You will have to work hard and smart to promote your web site so that potential customers can find it. At some point, you may decide to spend some advertising money, particularly for search engine–related pay-per-click ads. Still, it is possible to promote your site very effectively for absolutely no money, and this book shows you how.

SUPPORT SERVICES FOR THE WORLD WIDE WEB

Now that millions of people are connected to the Internet, a huge industry has grown up to support their activity. Web hosting companies and Web design companies are examples, as are software developers, computer repair companies, Web-based e-mail providers, search engine optimization companies, and the search engines themselves. Entrepreneurs who see a need are developing their own market niches, and the opportunities are unlimited.

NEWS AND GENERAL INFORMATION SITES

No doubt you already know about many web sites that offer news. For example, every big newspaper has its own web site, updated daily. Every television news department has its own site, with ongoing coverage of breaking news stories, and most radio station web sites include some news. National Public Radio's web site displays news stories, along with human interest and other articles. Even the home pages of Yahoo!, AOL, and MSN offer up-to-the-minute news.

You may not be aware of how much news is actually covered on the Internet by smaller, less famous reporting teams. For example, News of the Weird began as a column in underground newspapers, and has now migrated to the Web. Chuck Shepherd's coverage of truly bizarre news items appears on his web site blog every day except Sunday, along with his weekly column. Readers even have an open invitation to submit weird stories for inclusion on the site. Digg News is a participatory web site. Members register for free and may submit news stories from other sources. The Digg community then votes on the placement of stories on the site.

There are numerous sites that present and examine news from a religious viewpoint. Cross Walk (www.crosswalk.com) is a for-profit site that features news from a conservative Christian perspective. According to the "About Us" section of their site, "Our aim is to offer the freshest and most compelling biblically-based content to Christians who take seriously their relationship with Christ. . . . Within this framework, we work hard to provide timely, relevant, life-enhancing material from qualified, respected Christian sources. . . ."

A similar site, which bills itself as "politically incorrect, hard-hitting, Christian" is CrossAction News (www.crossactionnews.com). Christian Today (www.christiantoday.com) takes a gentler, ecumenical approach to the news. The Liberal Christian Network (http://www.hostdiva.com/liberalchristians/) offers news from a liberal Christian point of view.

Catholic World News (www.cwnews.com) describes itself as "an independent Catholic news service staffed by lay Catholic journalists, dedicated to providing accurate world news, written from a distinctively Catholic perspective." Jew Central (www.jewcentral.com) is a membership site whose content "is geared toward Jewish Professionals, no fluff, not the same old news and politics, just information to help you reach your goals." Islam Online (www.islamonline.net) is a membership site established by a group of Islamic scholars. It provides news of interest to Muslims, as well as other services such as counseling, advice forums, and articles on a variety of subjects.

Are you passionate about soccer? You can get all the latest soccer news at Soccer 365 (www.soccer365.com). Are you a video gamer? Computer and Video Games (http://www.computerandvideogames.com/) is a membership site with the latest news on games and the game business, as well as forums, reviews, and competitions. Ballroom dancers can find news of interest to them at Dancescape (http://www.dancescape.com).

Most of the sites just mentioned are supported by advertising and, in some cases, product sales. There are also paid special-interest membership sites. As you can see, there are many niches where you could find an appreciative audience eager for information on a vast array of subjects.

BLOGS

A blog (originally called a web log) is a diary of sorts, a series of comments published online and arranged to be read in reverse date order. The first blogs were simple Web pages. At the beginning of 1999, there were 23 blogs published on the Internet, according to one Web historian. During that year Blogger.com released software that made blogging easy for anyone to do, and in November 2000, the 10,000th blog was created. Today there are an estimated 90 million blogs on the web. Technorati (www.technorati.com) is a search engine specific to blogs, and it also publishes popularity rankings of blogs.

Originally blogs were personal musings, and that is often still the case. A great example of a personal blog that makes money is Heather Armstrong's Dooce (www.dooce.com). Armstrong began writing her blog in 2001. She writes about her life as a wife and mother, about her dog, and about her observations on life. Her husband, Jon, handles the technical side. By 2005, the site was generating enough advertising income to support the family.

Along the way, Armstrong added a new word to the lexicon. *Dooce* was a nonsense word she often used in place of *dude*, and the word became so associated with her she used it as the name of her blog. In 2002 she was fired from her job for blogging about her co-workers, and now when that occurs, the victim is said to have been *dooced*.

Today, blogs are also frequently published in conjunction with promoting business and professional interests. For example, musicians, performers, and athletes have their own blogs that help their fans know them better. Business owners write blogs on topics of interest to their customers or clients. Blogs can produce income through ad sales, including affiliate links (see the chapter, "A Closer Look at Affiliate Sales Sites") promoting products with links to sales pages, or indirectly by raising the profile of the business.

Since we have been talking about news, we must mention the news blogs—a true Internet phenomenon. Blogging has provided a platform for anyone with Internet access to write news and commentary.

As many news bloggers are not part of an institution, their credibility and accuracy are judged by their readers. Some news bloggers have a background in journalism, while others are avid amateurs.

A number of news bloggers have broken big stories initially ignored by the mainstream media. For example, liberal blogger Josh Marshal, of Talking Points Memo (www.talkingpointsmemo.com), spent several months researching the firing of U.S. Attorneys by the Department of Justice (DOJ) in the Bush administration. As the site continued to present new information, major media outlets also began to focus on the story. A few guys working in a rented room in a building in Manhattan lit the fuse on a story that eventually led to Congressional hearings.

News blogs represent all points on the political landscape. A popular conservative blog is The Anti-Idiotarian Rottweiler (http://www.nicedoggie.net/2007/) which proudly bills itself "The Most Annoying Right-of-Center Blog." An aggregate of Libertarian blogs can be found at http://libertarian.zebby.org.

Blogs have played an important role recently during times of natural disaster and war. After the deadly tsunami of December 2004, survivors and aid workers reported information via cell phone text messaging, and people throughout the world shared the information on their blogs. In the aftermath of Hurricane Katrina, Troy Gilbert, author of the GulfSails blog http://www.gulfsails.blogspot.com, kept the world apprised of the devastation and the eventual halting steps toward recovery. We recently interviewed Troy, and he told us his story:

I started GulfSails as kind of a joke for some sailing buddies here in New Orleans and the Gulf Coast—basically, I was just messing around with it, when Katrina reared her head. I have never evacuated for any hurricane and as I was preparing the house for the storm, I decided to start writing about the preparations. After the storm, I was able to post via cell phone until, amazingly, I got a landline phone working and was able to post full text and photos. (I also had a generator).

Long story short, I was one of only two bloggers on the ground in New Orleans throughout the storm and the aftermath and have been covered by

MSNBC, Washington Post, Times-Picayune, *et cetera. I'm even now in Wikipedia. I didn't even know that anyone was really reading it until Reuters got in touch with me by day three or so and asked what I thought about people reading it. I asked him who was reading. He replied, "The whole world." Needless to say, it knocked my socks off.*

Before the storm, I was trying my hand at freelance journalism. Since the storm, I am now starting to earn a living from it and will also have my first book published in the fall of 2008. I still have an interest in trying to get the blog published as a sort of Katrina memoir, but haven't yet decided on whether to tackle that or not.

Has it changed my life? Katrina changed everything, and I honestly think that without the release that I got from the blog, I would have lost my mind.

Early in the Iraq War, a 29-year-old Iraqi architect calling himself Salam Pax started the blog "Where Is Raed?" (http://dear_raed.blogspot .com). Salam Pax received wide attention in the United States and the United Kingdom, and his blog was adapted into a book. The Mesopotamian blog (http://messopotamian.blogspot.com), published in Iraq by Alaa, continues Pax's tradition with the intelligent commentary of another Iraqi citizen. A woman who calls herself Riverbend writes from a female perspective in http://riverbendblog.blogspot.com. In her description of herself in the first posting, she said simply, "I'm female, Iraqi, and 24. I survived the war. That's all you need to know. It's all that matters these days anyway." There are numerous blogs by Iraqis of all political points of view, and by soldiers of other countries. Many American military personnel publish their own blogs, although some have encountered censorship from their superiors.

Of course, you can go online and read any blog. But readers may also subscribe and receive updates to favorite blogs automatically. In Internet terms, blog updates are disseminated using *pull* technology initiated by the recipient (versus e-mail, which is disseminated using *push* technology and initiated by the sender). The technology used for disseminating blogs is RSS, an acronym for either *rich site summary* or *really simple syndication,* depending on which interpretation you accept.

Subscribing is easy—just press the "Subscribe" button (usually a big orange button) located in the column next to the blog text. To receive the updates, you must have a news reader, which is software that locates the updates and makes them accessible. Some news readers are accessed through a browser, and many more are available as free or paid downloads. Here is a list of popular news readers:

For Windows

> News Crawler (http://www.newzcrawler.com)
> Feed Demon (http://www.newsgator.com/home.aspx)
> Sage Firefox Plugin (http://sage.mozdev.org/)

For Mac

> Newsfire (www.newsfire.com)
> Net News Wire (www.newsgator.com)

Internet-Based

> Blog Lines (www.bloglines.com)
> My Yahoo! (www.yahoo.com)
> News Gator (www.newsgator.com)

The browser-based news readers allow you to access blog updates through any computer. The downloadable programs enable you to store the updates on your computer in the same way incoming e-mails are stored. The Internet Explorer 7 browser comes with an RSS reader already installed. You can learn much more about blogs in the chapter, "Make it Hypnotic!".

ENTERTAINMENT SITES

People surf the Internet as entertainment, and to find information about off-line entertainment. Sites that make viewers laugh and have fun are always welcome, and they offer good business opportunities as well. Following is an array of very different examples.

One of the funniest sites on the Internet, and one of the most exciting success stories, is Jib Jab (www.jibjab.com), the brainchild of brothers Gregg and Evan Spiridellis. The brothers started their digital media company in a Brooklyn garage in 1999, and for six years they struggled to stay afloat. Then, during the 2004 presidential election, they produced an animated digital cartoon called *This Land,* which hilariously, and equally, lampooned the candidates. The cartoon went viral. So many people heard about it and visited the site that their server crashed. The result was huge media attention, and ultimately an investment by a major venture capital firm. Today, the future of Jib Jab appears unlimited.

Aardman (www.Aardman.com) was developed by the animation company that rose to fame with the Wallace and Gromit characters. It features the low-key British humor that catapulted the series into movie stardom. If you are animator, a writer, a filmmaker, or a musician, your site could entertain visitors with your art.

Opus 1 Classical (www.opus1classical.com) provides database access to classical performances all over the world, along with the opportunity to purchase tickets to many events online. Commercial sites related to entertainment exist in all genres of music, literature, and art.

Naked Authors (www.nakedauthors.com) is the blog site of crime novel authors James Grippando, Patricia Smiley, Paul Levine, Jacqueline Winspear, James O. Born, and Cornelia Read. Although all of these writers (many of them award winners) have their own individual sites, they use the blog to talk about their work and work they admire. If you are a writer, or part of any group of friends with common interests, group blogs provide an interesting combination of voices for the reader to enjoy.

Indie Music Appreciation Group (www.indiemusicgroup.com) sponsors pages for 74 independent music artists, along with news about artists and recommendations. We know the number of artists is 74 because the site's owner, Doug Morris, does not accept advertising income, and his server space will not accommodate more pages. Occasionally he deletes one artist's page and substitutes another. Doug works at Wal-Mart in Joplin, Missouri, and he developed a passion for "Indie" music while recovering from a heart attack. For him, the site is a labor of love, and he wants to keep it that way. His example, however, highlights the possibilities for similar sites with a commercial orientation.

Astrology Zone (www.astrologyzone.com) is the web site of professional astrologer Susan Miller. At this site, you can read your monthly forecast (always upbeat and fun) and check your compatibility with friends and potential mates. The site has a community feel, and lots of content for those who like to check the stars. Income is derived from advertising, book sales, and membership options for subscribers.

Dark Fish (www.darkfish.com) is the site of Timothy J. Rogers, who has developed software to allow visitors to play board games online, against the computer. The games are Checkers, Reversi, Five Field Kono, Nim Skulls, Pentalpha, and Taxi. Rogers allows other site owners to license and use games for $200 each, which includes some customization.

Blue Sfear (www.bluesfear.com) is a site for artists who work in digital media. It includes tutorials and downloads of graphic arts programs, articles, resources, and a forum. The site is supported by advertising.

As you can see, there is some overlap between news sites and entertainment sites, and that is a perfect illustration of the interweaving of ways we as consumers, researchers, and viewers use the Internet. We surf to buy, to get information, and to have fun. If you as an entrepreneur can develop a site that will deliver in each of those areas, it will be successful!

AUCTION SITES

Many people have gotten their start doing business on the Internet through the online auction sites. This is particularly true of eBay, which continues to be the biggest and best known of the auction sites. Other types of Internet businesses can also find opportunities to grow using the auction sites. We've included an entire chapter on this subject—see A Closer Look at Online Auctions.

AFFILIATE SALES SITES

In the Internet world, an *affiliate* is a person who refers potential new buyers to a seller's site. If the referral makes a purchase, the seller pays the affiliate a portion of the proceeds of the sale. Many Internet businesses build a network of affiliates who help promote their products or services.

For example, Jillian offers an information product related to government grants for real estate. It is called *The New American Land Rush: How to Buy Real Estate with Government Money* (www.NewAmericanLand Rush.com). There are thousands of sites which offer training and other resources to real estate investors, and these sites are natural affiliates for the *Land Rush* product. Jillian has an affiliate manager whose job is to set up and maintain these relationships.

Joe has a number of products related to hypnotic writing (www .HypnoticMarketingInc.com) and maintains a business relationship with a separate company that markets the products through its extensive affiliate network. When one of our affiliates makes a sale for us, we pay them a commission. For our affiliates, making referrals to our products is a sideline, but still a lucrative part of their overall business.

Many entrepreneurs, however, are building big Internet businesses doing only this one thing: acting as affiliates selling other companies' products. These may be physical products or services. Because this is a proven, very viable business model, we have included an entire chapter on affiliate sales sites—see "A Closer Look at Affiliate Sales Sites."

SOCIAL NETWORKING SITES/FORUMS

It seems only natural that human beings will find opportunities to use the Internet for socializing, given the amount of time many people now spend online. Online forums are virtual conference rooms (or perhaps a coffee house would be a better analogy) where visitors gather to discuss topics of mutual interest. Forums originally appeared on the Internet in 1995, and there are now forums on every topic imaginable. A variety of software programs support forums, which are also sometimes referred to as message boards, discussion groups or boards, and bulletin boards.

The first social networking site was Classmates (www.classmates .com), which went online in 1995. Classmates helped old friends connect with one another, and the popularity of that concept fostered the development of a number of similar sites. Dating sites soon followed and became immensely popular. By 2004, $473 million was spent on Internet dating sites (Jupiter Research, quoted in USA Today, http://www.USAToday.com/tech/webguide/internetlife).

One of the most popular dating sites is e-Harmony (www .eharmony.com), founded by Neil Clark Warren. Californian Warren worked as a clinical psychologist and often counseled divorcing couples. He had a dream of helping people make better marital choices, and in 1992 he wrote a book called *Finding the Love of Your Life*. He developed a system of 29 areas of compatibility that allow a relationship to flourish. The system eventually received a patent. With the support of investors, eHarmony went online in 2000. Today this family-run business employs 130 people.

Plenty of Fish (www.plentyoffish.com) is a very different dating site. For one thing, it is completely free to its users. Founder Markus Frind first set the site up in 2003 as a casual project he could use to learn ASP.NET. Now the fifth-largest dating site in the world, Plenty of Fish receives 13 million page views every day, and Frind says it generates 300,000 successful relationships every year. Unlike the paid dating sites, the design of Plenty of Fish is extremely plain. However, the community of users is a very enthusiastic and active one that participates in operating the forums and hosting live parties where people can meet in person. As a result, Frind and his girlfriend operate the site without employees, from their apartment in Vancouver, British Columbia. The fact that the site is free does not mean Frind is not compensated. In fact, he has become a millionaire through Google AdSense ads (see the chapter, "A Closer Look at Affiliate Sales Sites").

A very popular site among young people is MySpace (www.myspace.com), which went online in 2003. The format of MySpace is typical of social networking sites. Users register for access, then create personal profiles detailing their age, gender, sexual orientation, relationship status, and preferences in politics, music, film, and hobbies. Networking happens through the building of "friends" lists. Every MySpace user has access to e-mail and instant messaging within the network.

During the past few years, an enormous social shift has taken place, as teenagers and young adults are forming more and more of their dating and friendship relationships through MySpace and similar sites. MySpace users are not all young and single, however. Many business owners, entertainers, and politicians own MySpace accounts and use them to generate interest in their offerings.

The first college networking site was Facebook (www.facebook.com), founded in 2004 by Harvard student Mark Zuckerburg as a way to make friends. Facebook soon grew to include colleges all over the world and became enormously popular among students. In September

2006, Facebook removed the restrictions on registration to allow anyone to become a member by joining a geographic network.

A simple illustration of the power of the social networking site is the story of how Erik Husa helped organize the Pierce County AIDS Walk. Eric was a student at Pacific Lutheran University in Tacoma, Washington, and at the time he had a network of 200 friends who had signed on to his Facebook account. He contacted them all and invited them to participate with him and to invite others. As a direct result of his Facebook networking, 167 people joined his team. "It's cheap and relatively effortless in making a large number of people aware of the event. . . . It's expandable beyond myself," said Eric as quoted in Megan Haley's article "Virtual Society" (http://www.plu.edu/scene/issue/2006/winter/features/virtual-society.html).

An even more dramatic and poignant demonstration of the power of social networking sites occurred during the writing of this book. In April 2007, a tragic shooting on the campus of Virginia Tech University took the lives of dozens of students and faculty. By the end of that day, 20,000 students were on Facebook at one time, consoling each other and remembering the victims.

SALE OF INFORMATION PRODUCTS

The statistics we have cited earlier in this chapter demonstrate a central truth of the Internet: People go online searching for information. The development and sale of information products of all types is a huge Internet business opportunity.

Both Joe and Jillian are consultants and do occasional work with clients. But over the years both of us have earned most of our income providing information to our readers. We both have a number of sales sites specific to each of our products.

Joe's products relate to marketing and to integrating spirituality into business and every aspect of life. Many people know Joe from the movie *The Secret* and from his spiritual best-sellers, *The Attractor Factor* (John Wiley & Sons, 2005) and *Zero Limits* (John Wiley & Sons, 2007).

When you visit his main site, www.MrFire.com, you will find Joe's fact-filled monthly newsletters; hundreds of articles; photos of his travels with his love, Nerissa; as well as his collection of cars (be sure and check out Francine, his hand-made 2005 Panoz Esperante GTLM). You can read his blog and have fun viewing his entertaining video blog. And, of course, you can also check out a wide variety of information products and purchase the ones you like.

Jillian's background is in counseling and consulting with businesses and nonprofits. Her site, www.GrantMeRich.com, offers information about the world of grants as well as her highly professional Grants Training Classes. You can learn there, purchase products, or enroll online.

Jillian frequently writes about real estate, and particularly how to take advantage of the thousands of available government grants and low-cost loans available to real estate investors. She's at work now on a book on the topic. You can learn much more (and see a brief video) at www.NewAmericanLandRush.com. Another site is www.DrJillian. com, where you can read about her classes on success and spirituality. You can also check out her other upcoming book, *The Other Secrets: Beyond the Law of Attraction*.

As you can see, we both create products and write about the things we know and about which we are passionate. In the chapter, "It All Begins with You," you did an exercise to identify your natural niche or niches. Using the conclusions you drew from that exercise, you can begin thinking about the possibility of creating your own information products. In the chapter "Create Your Own Information Products," you will learn all about how to easily produce an unlimited number and variety of information products. We also give you some tools to research the potential market before you create a product.

EDUCATION SITES

One substratum of information product sites is education sites. A number of businesses have been developed to offer all types of education and training over the Internet. An example is The Teaching Company (www.teach12.com), which offers university-level classes. Word 2 Word Language Resources (www.word2word.com) offers a database of language classes on the Internet. Free-Ed (www.free-ed.net) offers online classes from algebra to welding, absolutely free. Advanced Academics (www2.advancedacademics.com) offers accredited online high school classes. A variety of technical classes related to the Internet are available through eClasses (www.eclasses.org). Universal Class (www.universalclass.com) offers classes on a range of topics from accounting to crafts to performing arts, all at very affordable prices.

Both of us have offered online classes at different times. Jillian trains grant writers personally through her web site, www.GrantMeRich.com, and she has created freestanding educational modules for www .GrantsUniversity.com, a training site for nonprofit and social service agencies. Online classes are an excellent product in certain markets.

Our next guest expert, Rhea Perry, is committed to quality education. She has homeschooled all seven of her children, and she has made a career of providing entrepreneurial education to parents and family groups.

GUEST EXPERT ARTICLE

EDUCATING FOR ENTREPRENEURSHIP

Rhea Perry

If you have more than one child, you know what I mean. In every family, there is one kid that you just don't know what to do with.

Well, let me tell you what happened to mine.

About 20 years ago, I finally gave in to the pleas of my public school teacher husband and started educating our children at home. It was easy when there were just three. Now there are seven, plus three in heaven.

My oldest son Drew was never very academic but was always a good child who was ready to learn. By the time he was 14, I threw up my hands and told God, "If you want him to have an education, you'll have to give it to him."

It was almost as if I could hear God breathe a sigh of relief.

For the next several years, Drew managed our farm and studied the stock market. He loved farming but realized there was no money there unless you inherit an existing business.

He also decided that the stock market wasn't for him. We didn't consider that a failure; it was just part of the career elimination process.

Next he experimented with eBay and loved selling junk he found in the basement.

When he was 18, I took him to his first real estate investment conference and he instantly discovered his passion. Within three years, Drew met his first goal of purchasing or managing 21 houses by the time he was 21.

He also replaced my husband's income and met his second goal of bringing his dad home from corporate America. His dad was then able to care for his bed-ridden father, who lived with us for almost four years.

Now, at 25, Drew sells houses on eBay and teaches real estate investors how to create passive income by selling houses on eBay. He also recently married the girl of his dreams.

I now take my older children to conferences throughout the year to teach them society's ways instead of sending them out to learn life's lessons from their peers.

I continually look for mentors who meet the high standards I have for my children. And when I find some that meet my standards, I invite them to teach other families.

When Drew and I started learning together, I shared our success with my Yahoo! group at a one-day event. That event has developed into an annual family business conference that is now held in two locations every year—one on the east coast, one on the west.

Our keynote speakers have been Mark Victor Hansen; Troy McClain of NBC's *The Apprentice*; Sharon Lechter, co-author with Robert Kiyosaki of *Rich Dad Poor Dad*, and New York State Teacher of the Year John Taylor Gatto.

Our business is Internet-based. We promote our conferences through our web site and stay in touch with our readers through e-mail. At our family-friendly events, we encourage parents to take their children into the world of business and learn to become financially free together. The teens there haven't yet learned to fear failure, so they are still bold enough to actually do something with what the speakers teach.

I take my responsibility to bring mentors to families very seriously. I consider it an honor to be in a position to help parents learn to achieve financial independence and to teach their children to educate themselves for success!

(Continued)

> *Rhea Perry has educated her seven children since 1987. Her oldest son became a real estate investor when he was 18 and replaced his dad's income in just three years. Now at 25, he teaches real estate investors how to sell houses on eBay. Rhea hosts four conferences every year for families to learn about home business opportunities, including Internet-based businesses. For more information, visit www.RheaPerry.com.*

MEMBERSHIP SITES

One Internet business model, the paid membership site, offers an advantage unique in the world of the self-employed entrepreneur: a relatively predictable income. Membership sites generally provide members with the benefit of special access, either to information, services, or preferential pricing. Often, membership sites will offer both free and paid levels, so that members can decide how much they want to invest and receive. Buyers of this book can visit the book's web site, www.YourInternetCashMachine.com, and enjoy free access to a huge number of resources beyond those contained in these pages.

One membership site is Feminine Zone (http://femininezone.com), which features "The unique feminine perspective—all aspects of relationships, sex, mind and body, treated in a mature and intelligent way, with total frankness, by leading worldwide experts." Voices of Romance (www.voicesofromance.com) offers "romantic poetry, products, and relationship-building ideas." A&R Live! Hookup (www.armusic1.com) provides a vehicle to connect musical artists, songwriters, and producers with music industry insiders.

Membership sites are built using special software. Some companies offer their own membership site software combined with online hosting. In our opinion, the best, easiest, and most dependable software is available through www.amember.com. The customer purchases the software and has it installed on her own site. For more information on easy ways to build a membership site, see the chapter, "Set Up Your Web Site."

MULTILEVEL MARKETING/NETWORK MARKETING

One very popular business model is multilevel marketing (MLM), often called network marketing or direct sales (not all direct sales companies are set up on the multilevel model, but most are). In MLM, you join a company as an independent contractor to distribute the company's products or services. You then have two jobs: (1) sell the company's products and (2) recruit new distributors to work under you (in your *downline*). Your compensation is based on a percentage of the revenue earned by you and by those in your downline. You are probably familiar with some of the MLM companies, such as Avon, Mary Kay, and Tupperware. Other big ones include: Creative Memories, Electrolux, Herbalife, Mannatech, Pre-Paid Legal, Shaklee, Usana, and hundreds of others.

During the 1970s, Jillian went with her husband to an Amway presentation. They heard a glowing story of financial opportunity, and he was persuaded. They were young and looking for ways to make more money. She remained very skeptical, mostly because she could not picture herself asking friends and family members to buy anything from her. She knew she was not that kind of salesperson, and she knew her husband was not. Ultimately, like tens of thousands of other people, they ended up with a garage full of soap powder and household cleaners. Over the years they gave some away and used the rest. For a long time afterward, she dismissed the idea of MLMs.

The MLM business has changed for the better, however. In the 1980s, companies began to take over the handling of inventory and distribution. This change often lowered the initial cost of becoming a distributor, by lowering requirements for amount of inventory purchased. And in the 1990s, the growth of Internet business made it possible for MLM entrepreneurs to take the business out of their friends' living rooms and onto the World Wide Web. Now a network marketing businessperson can access an unlimited number of potential customers and downline distributors in the same way other Internet businesses reach their markets.

A variety of different organizational and compensation structures are used by these companies, and many of them are quite complex. It is important to analyze and fully understand the downline structure and payment plan before making any investment. It is wise to exercise due diligence prior to making a decision to join an organization.

The Federal Trade Commission (FTC) encourages people to be cautious in evaluating MLM opportunities. In April 2006, the agency proposed a new trade regulation rule, called the Business Opportunity Rule, which would require all companies offering business opportunities, including multilevel marketing companies, to provide concrete evidence to allow investors to evaluate the real likelihood and level of potential profits. It will probably be several years before that rule is finalized.

Varying portions of the money generated by many multilevel marketing companies are garnered through distributors buying into the business, rather than through product sales. If you are exploring the opportunity presented by an MLM company, be aware that a high cost to become a distributor, or a requirement to buy a significant amount of inventory, should be a red flag. In many such cases, your prospects of establishing a downline are slim and the company may collapse relatively quickly.

One problem with the MLM business model is that the distributor is not actually an owner of his own business. In many cases, the distributor is not permitted to represent other product lines, and the distributorship is contingent upon following company guidelines.

Multilevel marketing opportunities appeal to people in the same way all opportunities for self-employment do. They offer the possibility of financial and personal independence, and they may seem a safe haven for people who have lost jobs or feel the need to get out of an existing job. Moreover, MLM companies offer extensive emotional and business support through personal relationships and meetings.

In our opinion, this is a two-edged sword. Support and training are helpful when they are based on a factual premise. Much MLM support and training is still geared solely toward encouraging distributors to sell through personal contacts, and that simply does not work for most people. Few people can tolerate seeing their friends cringe as they push them to come into their downline. If you are interested in multilevel marketing, we suggest you look for a reputable company that does not restrict you to working only with them and that emphasizes the use of Internet business principles discussed in this book.

There are some excellent MLM companies. In fact, a dozen of them are publicly traded. The following guest expert article, by Paulie Sabol, discusses one of the new MLM companies, founded by respected entrepreneurs and firmly anchored in the best practices of Internet marketing. We also like this company because it allocates a portion of all its income to charitable giving.

GUEST EXPERT ARTICLE

GEOMETRIC GIVING: THE EASY WAY TO DONATE $1 MILLION A MONTH TO CHARITY

Paulie Sabol

Imagine writing a $1 million dollar check to charity. What would it take for you to be able to do that? How long would you have to work at your job for it? If you're like the average American, you earn roughly $35,000 a year. It would take over 28 years if you could save every dime.

Now imagine you have a burning desire to give residually, month after month, a million dollars a month. One way to be a million-a-month passive philanthropist is to save $240 million in a bank CD earning 5 percent and endorse the interest check to your charity. But clearly, saving that kind of money is far outside most people's abilities. However, you can still become this kind of giver though *geometric giving*.

Here's how it works, in three steps:

1. Select an enlightened affiliate marketing program. The product must be a membership like a book club or monthly professional development group.
2. Use the provided training system and affiliate tools designed to compound small efforts.
3. Commit to do your little part for up to two years.

The last step stops most people. While everyone would like to become a million-dollar giver, some aren't ready to commit to an effective system for two years because it starts off slowly.

Consider the program I'm using to do geometric giving through a $35/month book and personal development club. Of the $35 membership fee, one dollar is donated automatically and residually. It all starts with your dollar.

(Continued)

Now you might be wondering, how do you go from giving a dollar a month though your own membership to causing $1 million a month in giving?

Watch this. Say you learn how to use the system to share this book club with one new member each month—this is very doable even for absolute beginners. It grows while you're learning to use the system, until, by using this system yourself, you'd be responsible for $25/month of giving after just two years. But this is still a far cry away from $1 million per month, because when you depend solely on your own efforts, you're only using *linear* giving. The accompanying chart shows the results from linear growth.

Month	Number of Givers	Amount Given	Percent Increase
0	1 (You)	$ 1	N/A
1	2	$ 2	100%
2	3	$ 3	50%
3	4	$ 4	33%
4	5	$ 5	25%
5	6	$ 6	20%
6	7	$ 7	17%
. . .	. . .	. . .	. . .
22	23	$23	4.5%
23	24	$24	4.3%
24	25	$25	4.2%

Linear giving slows down the increase in giving month after month because members haven't learned how to compound their giving.

Now imagine both enrolling one additional member for $35/month, and also, introducing the new member to the systems and tools to do the same. As each new member recruits another, you achieve miracles. When you release your "do it all myself" obligation and allow others to learn to use the systems, geometric giving happens.

Check out the geometric giving chart.

Month	Number of Givers	Total Giving	Percent Increase
0	1 (You)	$ 1	N/A
1	2	$ 2	100%
2	4	$ 4	100%
3	8	$ 8	100%
4	16	$ 16	100%
5	32	$ 32	100%
6	64	$ 64	100%
7	128	$ 128	100%
8	256	$ 256	100%
9	512	$ 512	100%
10	1024	$ 1,024	100%
11	2048	$ 2,048	100%
12	4096	$ 4,096	100%
13	8192	$ 8,192	100%
14	16384	$ 16,384	100%
15	32768	$ 32,768	100%
16	75536	$ 75,536	100%
17	151072	$ 151,072	100%
18	302144	$ 302,144	100%
19	604288	$ 604,288	100%
20	1208576	$1,208,576	100%

And there you have it—a system to become a $1 million monthly giver in fewer than two years.

Because of the power this kind of giving has on the world, I encourage you to set the goal right now to be responsible for $1 million a month in charitable giving. And when you set that goal with me, something amazing happens. While the charity is making $1 million a month (or more), so are you. That's called *geometric earning*. You earn right along with the charity because the same system you used to grow your book club will also make you $1 for each member in your team.

And it's working. I just got off the phone with the owner of the book club membership. He called to congratulate me for being the fastest affiliate earner in the company's history. And what excited me is that also means I'm the fastest giver.

(Continued)

Of course, it's not really me, is it? You see, if it were about me, it would simply be a linear result. Geometric results require a team effort, and anyone who joins the team has the same opportunity to give and receive.

Paulie Sabol is the co-founder of MatrixMillionaires.com, a training program designed to help people become geometric learners, geometric givers, and geometric earners. Paulie has enlisted the support and team leadership of the world's best, including Mark Victor Hansen, Mike Filsaime, Donna Fox, Robert G. Allen, and many more enlightened business owners to create this system. If you are eager to learn to work just a little bit more to give a lot more money (and earn a lot more money), visit www.Books4People.com.

GAMBLING AND ADULT SITES

Although gambling and adult (often called *porn*) sites are not our area of the business, and it is outside the scope of this book to provide a guide to those niches, no chapter on Internet business models would be complete without mention of them.

In 1994, the first company to develop the software for online gambling and the online transfer of cash was Cryptologic, based in the Caribbean country of Antigua and Barbuda. Canada also had early gambling sites, which were regulated by an agency of the Canadian government. The United Kingdom, Australia, and Lichtenstein soon became home to other gambling sites.

American citizens, with broad access to the Internet, became early players. Online gambling has been technically illegal in the United States, however, except for pari-mutuel horse racing, which has been exempt from the law. A few states such as Nevada and North Dakota made attempts to legalize online gambling for their residents, but were deterred by the Department of Justice (DOJ).

In 1995 the Clinton administration, under international pressure from the World Trade Organization (WTO), promised to open access for U.S. citizens to international gambling sites. However, the subject has remained contentious over the years, largely because of the influence of two very different interest groups. Conservative religious and moral groups oppose legalized gambling of any kind. More significantly, American gambling businesses headquartered in Las Vegas and Atlantic City have encouraged the federal government to take a protectionist stance and keep offshore gambling sites unavailable to Americans.

In September 2006, the U.S. Congress passed the Unlawful Internet Gambling Enforcement Act (UIGEA) as part of the larger SAFE Ports Bill. President Bush signed the bill into law two weeks later. The law made it illegal for American citizens to make online credit card payments to gambling sites located outside the United States, and froze millions of dollars in pending payments. As part of the crackdown, several owners of offshore gambling sites have been arrested by American authorities and are being prosecuted. Fearing for their livelihood and businesses, many American owners of gambling sites have sold their companies to offshore buyers, or have relocated outside the United States.

In April 2007, the WTO issued a ruling that the American action was discriminatory and violated the organization's rules. The WTO further stated that if the ban is not lifted, sanctions may be applied. The original complaint against the United States originated in the Caribbean country of Antigua and Barbuda. Antigua and Barbuda may now theoretically request sanctions. For example, the WTO might withdraw overseas protections for United States trademarks and copyrights.

The position of the Bush administration has generally been to ignore WTO rulings with which it does not agree, so as of the time of writing this book, the outcome is unknown. Owners of offshore gambling sites report their business has rebounded. Some of them are allowing Americans to continue to play, in violation of the American law. Others have barred Americans. One of those sites, which is based in the United Kingdom and utilizes cutting-edge video technology to attract patrons, continues to see a growth rate of 50 percent per month.

Joseph Kelly, professor of business law at State University of New York (SUNY) in Buffalo, believes that online gambling will eventually be legal in the United States. Quoted in www.NetworkComputing. com, Kelly said, "The panic created by the DOJ's actions will eventually subside, new legislation will be passed, and we'll see a regulated industry emerge. . . . The notion that you can put a definitive stop to online gambling is a ludicrous one."

Adult web sites have been a huge business since the inception of the World Wide Web in 1991. Sex is the third most frequently searched subject on the popular search engines, according to 2005 research by Cecil Adams of www.StraightDope.com (the top-five list is music, travel, sex, games, and eBay). The ability of consumers to access adult material in the privacy of their own homes has proven a substantial boon to that market, as have technological developments such as file sharing, streaming media, and live webcams. According to statistics presented on www.TopTenReviews.com, worldwide revenue from pornography during 2006 totaled at least $97 billion. The web site estimates that more than $3 million is spent every second on Internet porn. The greatest number of adult films and photographs offered through the Internet are produced in the United States. The biggest consumer is China, where the market was $27.4 billion in 2006. U.S. consumers spent $13.3 billion, South Korea $25.7 billion, and Japan $20 billion.

Interestingly, the Internet porn industry blazed trails that mainstream site owners have followed. For example, Ron Levi, owner of www .Cybererotica.com, pioneered the development of pay-per-click banner advertising in 1996. Levi also developed productivity clicks, paying affiliates for unique hits (hits from individual computers; each computer has its own IP address). In 1997, Levi developed an affiliate program in which the level of payment to affiliates was tied to the traffic generated.

Double opt-in e-mail programs, the state-of-the-art method used today to protect against spam (and to protect site owners against accusations of spamming), was also developed by Levi. In addition, Cybererotica developed a counter to put on sites and tracked traffic statistics, including the source of traffic to the site, search terms used, and browsers used by visitors.

Resource Page

Summary of topics discussed in this chapter:

Now that you've decided to start an Internet business, the next step is to choose a business model. In this chapter, we examined possible models:

- ☛ Bringing an off-line business online.
- ☛ Sales of physical products.
- ☛ Support services for the World Wide Web.
- ☛ News and general information sites.
- ☛ Blogs.
- ☛ Entertainment sites.
- ☛ Auction sites.
- ☛ Affiliate sales sites.
- ☛ Social networking sites and forums.
- ☛ Sale of information products.
- ☛ Education sites.
- ☛ Membership sites.
- ☛ A brief history of gambling and adult sites, and some of the technologies that are now used by mainstream Internet business.

Our guest experts write about taking business online, teaching entrepreneurship, and a cutting-edge MLM.

Go to www.YourInternetCashMachine.com to learn more about business models and how to participate in www .Books4People.com. You will also find interviews with our guest experts. Claim your free membership now!

A CLOSER LOOK AT ONLINE AUCTIONS

On Labor Day 1995, a young programmer named Pierre Omidyar launched a social experiment that irrevocably changed the face of business. Initially he called it Auction Web, but two years later it was renamed eBay. It was designed as a web site community in which every participant had equal access to the basic tools of buying and selling online. Omidyar wondered, "What would happen within a marketplace if everyone had equal access to information and tools? Would a level playing field enable individuals to compete alongside big businesses? What if members managed their own transactions and accountability?" At the heart of eBay was Omidyar's belief that most people are essentially trustworthy.

The experiment was an unprecedented success. Today over 200 million people throughout the world buy and sell on eBay. eBay has provided occasional income to individuals, supported the creation of numerous small businesses, and launched multimillion-dollar companies. Dozens of competitors have joined the marketplace, notably Yahoo! Auctions, Bidz.com, Amazon, ePier, OnlineAuction.com, Auction.com, and uBid.com. Many stars of the Internet marketing world got their start selling on eBay.

As you can see, selling items on the auction sites is a business in its own right, and millions of people are earning a living doing so. However, even if you establish an Internet business using your own web site, there are ways to use the auction sites to promote your products and build your list of customers. We discuss that later in this chapter.

If you like the idea of launching your Internet career in a structured environment, with instantly accessible support, the online auction sites may be for you. If you are a collector of any type, or if in your heart of hearts you just love to buy and sell, the online auctions will be exciting and satisfying. Another significant benefit is the quick cash return. You can pull something out of your attic, or come across a find at your local Goodwill, post it on the auction site, and sell it three days later. Because eBay is the largest online auction site, and continues to be rated best for users, this chapter focuses on eBay and its policies and possibilities. It is a good place to begin; then, when you have mastered selling on eBay, you may want to try your luck on some of the other auction sites.

GETTING STARTED ON eBAY

The keys to having happy customers on eBay and getting excellent feedback are simple: accurate descriptions, clear photographs, careful packaging, and prompt shipping. Setting up an account on eBay is the first step in getting started. If you have already made a purchase on eBay, you have an account, and you can utilize that same account as a seller. If not, here are the steps to follow:

1. At www.eBay.com, click on the "Register" link at the very top of the page.
2. Enter your contact information and personal data.
3. Enter your e-mail address. This is the address eBay will use to communicate with you, and they must be able to verify the address.
4. Enter your debit or credit card information and your checking account information. All your personal data will be encrypted by SSL encryption software, which provides a high level of security. However, if you prefer not to provide financial information, eBay does offer an alternative process called ID Verify.
5. Read the eBay user agreement and the privacy policy, and note your acceptance. These are legal documents that set forth your

relationship with eBay and outline the services and costs involved in listing and selling on eBay.

6. Create a user ID, password, and a secret question to be used if you forget your password. If you already have an idea what type of products you plan to sell, it would be good to select a user ID related to those products. For example, if you plan to sell antique dolls, include a reference to antique dolls as part of the name you choose. You can change an existing user ID, but not more frequently than every 30 days.

7. Check your e-mail for a registration notice from eBay, then follow the instructions to confirm and complete your registration.

It is possible to have more than one account on eBay, as long as the accounts have different user IDs and different e-mail addresses. If at a later time you decide to have only one account, you can then merge the accounts.

An important component in the success of eBay is the feedback function. Every buyer and every seller is requested to leave written feedback on her experience with the other party. Positive feedback increases the buyer's level of comfort, offering some confidence that the seller will deliver as promised. When you begin selling on eBay, potential buyers will look at your feedback score and may also go and read individual feedback comments. So whether you are buying or selling, it is very important to conduct each transaction with competence and integrity.

Sellers on eBay incur two fees. The first is the insertion fee, charged when an item is listed. The insertion fee varies according to the selling price of the item. The second is the final value fee, incurred only when an item has sold. The final value fee varies according to the final sale price of the item. For complete information regarding eBay fees, visit: http://pages.eBay.com/help/sell/fees.html.

PayPal, a subsidiary of eBay, is the payment method most commonly used by eBay sellers. PayPal allows your buyers to use either their own PayPal accounts or a debit or credit card to pay for their purchases in a secure online environment. If you do not yet have a PayPal account, you will want to set one up at www.PayPal.com. You may at some time in the future decide to set up your own merchant account and accept cards directly, but that is not necessary if you have a PayPal account.

Of course, PayPal does charge a small fee for each transaction, and those fees, added to the eBay insertion and sales fees, reduce your bottom-line profit. Some sellers choose to accept only checks or money orders. If you decide to go that route, I would recommend you tell your buyers in advance that merchandise will be shipped only after the checks have cleared. Keep in mind, however, that eBay buyers are accustomed to receiving merchandise they have purchased quickly so restricting transactions to checks or money orders will limit your number of bidders.

To begin selling on eBay, go to www.eBay.com and click on the "Sell" link. This will take you to the Sellers main page, where you can list your items as well as accessing a variety of helpful tools. But before you jump into the sales side, we recommend you spend some time touring eBay and learning your way around. The "Help" link at the top of eBay's home page will lead you to extensive and very useful information. Also, under "Community" you can find a number of member-to-member forums, news resources, and a community calendar of events.

There are four ways to sell products on eBay: regular online auctions, which are discussed extensively here; buy it now (BIN); live auctions; and in an eBay Store.

At the time an item is listed for auction, the seller is given the option of specifying a fixed price. A customer then has the opportunity to buy the item at any time during the auction period, stopping the auction. As you can readily see, there are plusses and minuses to setting a BIN price. By doing so, you may be putting a ceiling on the selling price. However, you are also allowing impulse buyers to make an immediate purchase at a price that guarantees you a profit. Once the first bid is offered on the item, the BIN price option disappears from the sales description page. Sellers often combine a reserve price—a hidden minimum selling price—with the BIN option.

Live auctions are a service provided by eBay to auction houses. Licensed auctioneers can list up to 10,000 lots per catalog, at an insertion fee of $1,500 per catalog, as of the time of this writing. There is also a final value fee of 5 percent of the final sales price for each successful lot. To learn more about Live Auctions, go to www.eBaylive auctions.com.

Setting up an eBay store allows you to leverage the tremendous traffic enjoyed by the auction site (close to 40 million visitors per month) in your own permanent storefront. eBay store items can remain online up to 90 days, and listing fees are less than the insertion fees for auction items. For a small monthly fee, you can open an eBay store, provided you have a minimum feedback score of 20 and a PayPal account or an ID Verify listing. When you name your eBay store, be keyword savvy. Choose two or three keywords that are likely to be searched by your potential buyers. To create your eBay store, go to www.stores.eBay.com, then click on the orange "Open a Store" button on the right.

WHAT TO SELL?

Deciding what to sell on eBay is a key component in your eventual success. For you, the decision may be obvious. Perhaps you love furniture, vintage fashion, military surplus, or art, and you have some resources for buying at prices well below market. Perhaps you are a collector of objects that will interest your fellow collectors throughout the world. If you have a personal passion, that's a great place to begin building an online auction business.

If you are not a collector, consider the activities you enjoy. There are potential products associated with your career, your hobbies, or your leisure activities. Aside from the pleasure you will get buying and selling the products you select, your buyers will appreciate your knowledge and experience.

A dizzying variety of items are sold on eBay every day, from beautiful antiques to modern electronics, from cars to real estate. Electronics, computer-related items, and cooking and kitchen items are reliable sellers in online auctions. Many sellers have built healthy businesses selling books, particularly coffee-table books. Jewelry, antique as well as new, is a huge market. Presently, the largest category on eBay is Business and Industrial Materials and Equipment. Many eBay merchants resell used items purchased at flea markets, garage sales, and thrift stores. Of course, eBay businesses are not limited to any one category, and many sellers do not specialize in a particular type of merchandise. Instead they look for good purchasing opportunities and sell anything they believe will generate a healthy profit. To see which items are the most searched for on eBay at any given time, go to http:// pulse.eBay.com.

Finally, you can create your own products. Some people sell original artwork, or crafts ranging from blankets to furniture to jewelry. Writers sell e-books, and software designers sell their software programs. Many eBay sellers have established viable businesses creating products to be used by other eBay merchants, such as eBay account management programs.

In deciding what to sell, and in selecting items to buy and resell, it is useful to understand the curve of supply and demand, both in the retail world and on auction sites. Economists have identified four phases in the life cycle of products: the introductory phase; the in-season retail phase (when the product is easily available in most retail stores); the end-of-life phase (when a new model is about to be introduced, and retail price reductions are common); and the liquidation phase.

The introductory phase is the part of the life cycle of a product when the demand is highest. You are probably familiar with the annual frenzy to purchase hard-to-find toys around Christmas. When new toys or computer systems are introduced in October or November, many eBay sellers buy up the available stock. Then, when retail stores are sold out, the eBay sellers list their stock in online auctions. Recognizing the incredible response of online auction buyers to new products, some manufacturers now introduce their new products on eBay first, before providing stock to retail stores.

All products have an introductory phase, which may last a few weeks or a few months. New clothing designs, for example, are introduced into the marketplace a couple of months in advance of their actual season. Thus summer clothes begin to appear in stores as early as February, and sweaters and jackets in August. Televisions and other electronics usually remain in the introductory phase a few months, until newer, improved models appear. In the case of automobiles, new models appear once a year, and the introductory phase lasts about nine months.

By the time a product has reached the liquidation phase, new models are already on the floor. Manufacturers and retail stores make every effort to get rid of their merchandise prior to this phase. For eBay sellers, the liquidation phase presents a potential moneymaking opportunity, because eBay buyers are all bargain hunters at heart. Many of those buyers would prefer to get a good product at a great price, rather than paying full retail for a product in its in-season retail phase. In fact, a number of eBay merchants specialize in offering liquidation merchandise. However, there are several factors that must be carefully weighed every time you decide to sell liquidation items.

The first consideration is demand. Before you purchase products in the liquidation phase, be sure there is still a market demand for the products. Do not buy fad products whose desirability has already peaked and probably passed. Do not buy products that did not sell successfully during their earlier phases. The best products to sell during the liquidation phase are those with popular brand names. Always research and determine how much of the product is already available on eBay, and avoid introducing more of a product into an already crowded market niche. That would bring prices down, perhaps below your ability to make a profit. One rule of thumb for larger merchants is to avoid buying more than 10 percent of the available quantity of the product.

The second consideration is your cost of goods. Cost is always important, of course, but it is of primary consideration at this point in the product life cycle. You must buy very low to profit from products during the liquidation phase. One final note on this subject: If you come across a great purchase price, you may be tempted to overbuy, but always remember, you do not want to get stuck with product after the demand has disappeared.

PRICING

One of your most important decisions regards pricing your auction items. It is useful to do some research before you decide. To research the history of similar items sold on eBay, go to the eBay "Advanced Search" page at http://search.eBay.com/ws/search/AdvSearch. Enter the keyword or item name that most closely matches the items you have to sell. Choose the appropriate category. Check the box that says "Completed Listings Only." Under the "Sort By" drop-down list, select "Ending Soonest." This search will bring up items similar to yours and display their actual selling prices.

We also recommend using Google for pricing research. Go to Google.com and enter into the "Search" box the keyword and item name. This will bring up every similar item for sale anywhere on the

Internet, including individual sellers through CraigsList (www.craigslist
.com) and other auction sites. For new or nearly new items, the list
will include the manufacturer, various retail stores, and sites such as
Shopping.com and Amazon.

The information you glean from this research is only a starting
point, of course. eBay shoppers are looking for a bargain, so you want
to price your item accordingly. Your strategy is to avoid losing money
on an item while encouraging vigorous bidding.

Some sellers choose to set a reserve price, which is the minimum
price at which they will part with the item. Auctions utilizing a
reserve price work exactly like regular auctions, except that the high
bidder must offer an amount at or above the reserve price in order to
win the auction. Reserve price auctions ensure the seller will not lose
money on items offered for auction. Bidders can see on the sales
page that there is a reserve price, but they do not know the amount
of the reserve.

Reserve price auctions do cost the seller extra; the eBay listing
price for reserve price auctions is tied to the amount of the reserve. If
you employ a reserve price auction and the item fails to sell, you can
still e-mail the highest bidder and offer to sell the item at that bidder's
offer price. A better tactic is to simply set the lowest acceptable price
as your bottom line, thus saving yourself the reserve price fee and still
protecting yourself against losing money. Many eBay customers sur-
veyed state they will not bid on auctions with a reserve price.

Some sellers start all auctions with "$1NR" pricing, which means
an opening bid of only $1.00 with no reserve price. While this pricing
structure may generate lots of bids, it carries a high risk that the final
bid will be less than the cost of the item auctioned. You may choose
to use this structure to foster initial interest in your business, but it is
not a viable tactic over time.

Statistics show that approximately 40 percent of items sell the first
time they are listed. If an item fails to sell, you can elect to relist the
item at a later time without paying a new insertion fee, under three
conditions. First, it must be less than 30 days since the closing date of
the first auction. Second, the first auction must not have been a *Dutch
auction* (explained in a moment), and you must not have received any
bids on the item. Third, if you held a reserve price auction, you must
not have received any bids that met the reserve price specified.

If no one met your reserve price (if one was specified), if the winning bidder failed to pay, or if you have an identical item but did not include it originally as part of a Dutch auction, you can make a *second chance offer*. Second chance offers can be made up to 60 days after the end of the sale. There is an eBay process for second chance offers. Go to your "My eBay" page, then to "Sold Under All Selling," click the "Action" menu, then click "Send a Second Chance Offer." These second chance offers are covered under eBay's buyer protection program. eBay does not charge sellers a second insertion fee for second chance offers.

Sometimes a seller has one or more identical items for sale at the same time. The seller can then employ a Dutch auction. In Dutch auctions, the seller sets a minimum acceptable sales price. Bidders offer that amount or more, and at the end of the auction, the top bidders win the items available. For example, if there are six items, the six top bidders win them. However, these winning bidders all pay the same price, namely the lowest winning bid that exceeds the minimum acceptable sales price.

If you decide to sell cars, car parts or auto accessories on eBay, you can do so at www.motors.eBay.com. Be aware that most states have laws governing the number of cars an unlicensed individual can sell in any given period. Check the laws in your state to ensure you are in compliance. You will also need to research the law in the buyer's state regarding title transfer. A significant number of cars sold on eBay are purchased by buyers in other parts of the country, so you may want to offer shipping (paid for by the buyer). A resource used by many eBay sellers is Dependable Auto Shipping, at http://www.dasautoshippers.com.

You can also list real estate on eBay. Property listings can be posted for 30 days or for 90 days. There is a significant insertion fee, but no selling fee is due at sale. To list real estate on eBay, go to http://pages.eBay.com/realestate, then go down the page and click on "Buyer and Seller Guides."

BUYING FOR RESALE ON AUCTION SITES

In the beginning, many eBay sellers offer items from around the house, such as outgrown toys or clothing, or kitchen items. Many sellers also haunt garage and rummage sales. Thrift stores such as Goodwill and Salvation Army, and discount stores such as Big Lots, are another good source of products. Going-out-of-business sales and out-of-season sales frequently offer very low prices on merchandise that can be resold on eBay. And, of course, you may find great deals on items to resell in eBay auctions!

There are many web sites that offer periodic bargains:

- *Closeout.net* (www.closeout.net) is an affiliate site that acts as a portal to many other closeout and surplus sales sites.
- *Comp USA* (www.compusa.com) is a retail store whose web site features wholesale prices and auctions. At the website, click "Auctions" to review these.
- *Gordon Brothers* (http://www.gordonbrothers.com/industry/content.cfm?id=wsale) purchases and resells wholesale lots of overstocks, closeouts, and cancelled sales.
- *Genco* (www.genco.com) provides product management services to 122 different customers in retail, manufacturing, and government. They offer retail surplus and second chance deals through eBay. You can get the direct link to their sales through the Genco site.
- *Liquidity Services, Inc.*, is a NASDAQ-traded company that operates the following web sites:
  - www.liquidation.com
  - www.wholesale411.com
  - www.gowholesale.com
- *Overstock.com* offers bulk items at wholesale prices. Go to the Overstock web site (www.overstock.com) and click the tab marked "Other Stores."
- *Tech Liquidators* (www.techliquidators.com) is affiliated with a technology retailer. They sell closeout items, returns, and salvage. They estimate 50 percent of their return items are usable, and only 10 percent of their salvage items.
- *Surplus.net* is a site that knows which keywords its clients are using. On its web site (www.surplus.net), the company's self-description is "surplus liquidation overstock closeout salvage imports exports." We can't do better than that.

Technology and other manufacturers also offer occasional closeout sales. In addition, many successful eBay sellers have built businesses importing and selling products from other countries.

PROMOTING YOUR AUCTIONS

To be effective in attracting customers, your auction sales page for each item must contain three components: a good headline; a clear, full, and accurate description; and excellent images. We recommend that you spend some time reading the chapter, "Make it Hypnotic!," then use some of that great copywriting advice to write your eBay headlines and descriptions. Remember, your item description is your sales copy.

Studies show 80 percent of eBay shoppers use the eBay search engine function. Spend some time selecting the most popular and descriptive keywords for your items, and make sure you list items in the most appropriate category.

As an eBay seller, you will benefit from having an "About Me" page displayed on the eBay web site. To create your page, go to http://pages.eBay.com/community/aboutme.html.

While getting started selling on auction sites requires very little initial cash outlay, we do encourage you to invest in a decent digital camera, and practice with lighting and backgrounds to produce the clearest photographs possible. It is slightly less expensive to list an item without a photograph, but doing so will eliminate the majority of potential bidders.

SHIPPING

On your sales page, you can select a single shipping method or offer one of several. Usually, sellers specify that buyers are responsible for the cost of shipping. If you are shipping a fragile or extremely valuable item, it is a good idea to mandate that the buyer pay for shipping insurance. Many eBay sellers utilize the post office Priority Mail service. The U.S. Postal Service (USPS) provides free Priority Mail shipping boxes, which can be ordered from the postal service web site (www.usps.com) or picked up at your local post office. Other sellers use FedEx or United Parcel Service (UPS). FedEx and UPS have always offered pickup service directly from businesses, and the Post Office has recently added that service.

Many sellers purchase merchandise from manufacturers or wholesalers that offer drop-shipping. You as a seller offer an item at auction. When it sells, you notify the wholesaler, which ships it to the buyer. The benefits of working with a drop-shipper are twofold. First, you do not need to buy inventory in advance. Second, you are not responsible for shipping. Some of the companies offering drop-shipping include:

☛   Doba.com was established to serve online merchants by supply-
ing and shipping merchandise (http://www.doba.com).

☛   Drop Ship Design supplies over 100,000 products to merchants
in the United States and the United Kingdom (www.dropship
design.com).

☛   MegaGoods.com is a wholesaler and drop-shipper of home
electronic and household items (www.megagoods.com).

In addition to the companies listed here, you can research other possibilities through Google. Keep in mind, however, that in the past some sellers have encountered serious problems selling products for which they could not provide fulfillment, when the drop-shippers they trusted failed to perform. Make sure you are dealing with a reputable company.

TIMING YOUR AUCTION

As a seller, you can choose how long you would like an auction to last. The options offered by eBay are one day, three days, five days, seven days, and ten days. (Real estate auctions are the exception; they last either 30 or 90 days.) Seven days is the duration most commonly employed. The seven-day auction gives buyers plenty of time to get interested in the product and provides time for potential buyers to find the product and drive up the bidding to a higher final sale price. Of course, you will want to experiment and determine for yourself which auction duration is best for your particular business.

Standard wisdom among sellers holds that auctions should end on a weekend, so that potential buyers can track items during the week, then make actual buying decisions on Saturday or Sunday, when they have time to shop. Statistics show the highest concentration of eBay customers shop online between 8 P.M. and midnight, Eastern time. From Thanksgiving through Christmas, noon to 3 P.M. is also a busy shopping time. Since most eBay customers view auctions in the order of those ending soonest, it makes sense to have your auctions approach their close when the most people are searching for your items.

THE PATH OF THE POWERSELLER

You may have already decided your intended goal is to build a big business on eBay, or you may come to that realization gradually. Thousands of eBay sellers have succeeded in achieving the status of *PowerSeller*. Ebay has defined five levels of PowerSellers, as follows:

Level	Monthly Sales
Bronze	$ 1,000
Silver	$ 3,000
Gold	$ 10,000
Platinum	$ 25,000
Titanium	$150,000

In order to be designated a Bronze level PowerSeller, you must sell $1,000 or more per month for three consecutive months, and to retain this status, you must continue to sell at or above this level. Your account with eBay must be in good standing and your fees paid. You must have at least 100 feedback entries, and 98 percent or more must be positive. In order to move to the next level, you must go through the same steps. For example, to move from Bronze to Silver, you must sell $3,000 or more each month for three consecutive months, and so on.

Invitations are sent to new PowerSellers once monthly. When you receive your invitation, be sure to opt in to receive e-mail communications for PowerSellers. eBay has established a special portal for Power-Sellers with access to advanced selling information. If at any time your sales fall below the minimum required level, eBay gives you 30 days grace to come back into compliance. Should you know in advance you will be taking a hiatus from selling, perhaps for a vacation or a planned surgery, notify eBay in advance to protect your PowerSeller status.

Merchants who have achieved PowerSeller status receive a special welcome kit from the CEO and an official certificate of achievement. PowerSellers may display a special logo in their listings and next to their eBay name on search results. They are also entitled to other special benefits such as PowerSeller business card and letterhead templates and merchandise to wear or give to customers. Perhaps the best benefit is access to the PowerSeller discussion board, where you can share experiences and learn from eBay's best performers.

TREAT IT LIKE A REAL BUSINESS

You may be running your eBay business in your pajamas, but it's real business nonetheless. And in a real business, it's important to know where you stand financially. Is your business successful? How much money are you really making? We're not talking about sales here but your bottom-line profits.

Once you understand your statistics, you can do strategic planning for growth. We recommend you compute these statistics monthly, quarterly, and annually. Here are some simple formulas to provide you a snapshot of the status of your business:

Gross sales—total sales, before deduction of expenses and non-paying sales.

Total expenses—the total of the cost of goods, eBay fees, PayPal fees, credit card fees, shipping and handling, rent, labor, and so on.

Net profit—total sales, less all expenses and nonpaying sales.

Average sales price—total of all gross sales, divided by the total number of items sold.

Nonpaying bidder rate—number of bidders who do not pay divided by the total number of bidders.

Sales closure rate—number of items sold, divided by number of items listed. This figure will show you what percentage of items you list actually sell.

With the information provided by these statistics, you can determine which figures need adjustment. For example, do you need to reduce your expenses? Perhaps you need to find a cheaper source of merchandise. If your rent and labor costs are disproportionately high, perhaps you need to list and sell more items to bring them into balance. Once you have a clear picture of the current financial status of your business, you can establish incremental goals for the future. What will it take to help your business grow in both gross sales and net profits?

BELLS AND WHISTLES

Following are some of the most popular tools currently being utilized by eBay sellers to automate the listing process and enhance sales, beginning with the tools offered by eBay itself:

Ebay's own desktop listing and sales management tools are Seller's Assistant and Seller's Assistant Pro (http://pages.eBay.com/sellers_assistant). The basic version provides a listing tool, tracking tool, and e-mail management, and costs $9.99 the first month. The professional version is geared toward high-volume and business sellers; it includes sales management and bulk listing software, along with post-sales assistance. Cost begins at $24.99 per month.

Another eBay product, Turbo Lister (http://pages.eBay.com/turbo_lister/), allows the seller to create bulk listings, to retain listing details for future use, to save default values, to easily create duplicate listings and descriptions, and to schedule listings to begin at a specific future time. Blackthorne Basic and Blackthorne Pro (http://pages.eBay.com/blackthorne) are additional tools offered by eBay.

Auction Lynxx (www.auctionlynxx.com) provides an intuitive interface that cross-promotes each of the seller's items listed for auction. The software automatically updates the cross links whenever an auction begins or ends.

Auction Bytes (www.auctionbytes.com/cab/pages/ams), an independent trade publication for online merchants, lists a variety of merchant tools that can be utilized on eBay, Overstock.com, Yahoo!, Amazon and others.

Auction123.com (www.auction123.com/) offers tools for sellers on eBay Motors, Auto Trader (www.autotrader.com) and Cars.com (www.cars.com).

HOW TO LEVERAGE eBAY

Auction sites can also be a great way to build your Internet reputation and drive traffic to your other Internet business sites. Although eBay rules prohibit including outside links in your auction listings, you can give the name of your business, and direct visitors to your eBay "About You" page, where you can include a link to your other sites. It is also possible to buy eBay classified ads, which may contain outside links and phone numbers. Classified ads cost $10 for 30 days and can be purchased to run up to 90 days.

Our next guest expert began his Internet career on eBay. Now he trains Internet business owners to use eBay to build a much bigger online presence.

GUEST EXPERT ARTICLE

eBAY AND BEYOND

Jim Cochrum

I was honored when Jillian asked me to contribute an article to *Your Internet Cash Machine*.

Isn't the visual image of money spilling off the Internet into your bank account exciting? The concept behind the book you are reading now couldn't be a better fit for my philosophy and experience on the Internet. I see the Internet as my personal cash machine. In this article I share the key principle that has brought automated-cash-machine-type success to me and many other entrepreneurs I know.

My background and foundation are on eBay, but don't mistake me for one of the die-hard eBay sellers who spend 60 hours per week running a sell-collect-ship-repeat business. I admire people who use eBay to make a living in *any* fashion, but my philosophy on eBay is simple.

If you are like 99 percent of the Internet marketers I meet, you need to learn to see eBay differently than you do now. You need to see eBay as a *lead-generating machine* that can put a constant stream of paying customers into your automated sales funnel. If your perception of eBay is that it is hard work or not worth it, then you are simply uninformed.

A goal of mine since the mid 1990s has been to create multiple automated income streams to live on so I could have free time to spend at home with my family. We like long vacations, playing at empty parks in the middle of the week, going to the zoo on Tuesdays, and hitting Disney theme parks during the slow off-season. A traditional job would make this all impossible.

(Continued)

Since 2002, I've been blessed to enjoy the lifestyle that only the Internet can offer. I now have multiple Internet income streams. At last count I had about 35 income streams, none of which require daily attention. It gets seriously difficult to keep track of how many streams there are when they are all so automated.

Some of my income streams are as small as $100 to $200 per month. Some streams are significantly larger. Add them all up and I'd have to work 60-hour weeks as the CEO of a major corporation to get the same income results—and I wouldn't get to be home with my family during the day. Some weeks I work as few as 10 hours.

For me, the foundation of all my success has been eBay and I'm honestly *not* working hard at it. Am I creative about my business? Yes. Am I working hard? No.

I'm happy to share the key strategy that has been the foundation not only for my success but, based on the testimonials I get all the time, it's worked for hundreds of others as well.

May I tell you about a book I wrote? I've sold tens of thousands of copies of an e-book I wrote several years ago (and have updated five times since) that tells the whole story of how I use eBay as a lead-generation machine, but in this article I'll do my best to sum it all up for you. The book is titled *The Silent Sales Machine Hiding on eBay* and is *only* sold at SilentSalesMachine.com.

The "silent sales machine" technique that I use allows me to set up multiple hands-free income streams by harnessing the power of eBay. It does take a little effort to get the first stream established, but you will be well rewarded for your efforts. I set up my first silent sales machine in less than a week from start to finish. It started making me predictable steady cash with very little monthly maintenance. My time was then free for me to create more income streams on or off eBay. In my book I go into step-by-step detail on how I did it, but in this article my only goal is to convince you of the power of these ideas.

The key to my success was when I realized the power of *information* combined with eBay. Information *is* power. If you want to establish loyal lifetime customers, the strategy is easy. Give customers the *exact* information they are looking for *right when they want it*.

We live in a day and time where people are sick of being interrupted and having random products and information pushed on them—but at the same time, those same people want instant free information on topics that are of interest to them. Grasp those two facts and I'll show you a gold mine of opportunity.

If you can supply relevant, timely, and in some cases free information to someone on the Internet, you've won them over, possibly for life. If you try to force that information on a random audience, though, you'll certainly see frustrating results. The obvious question then becomes, how do I get in front of prospects who want information, and what information do I give them?

Unless you are a search engine optimization guru, you should be checking out the second-largest search engine on the planet. It's called eBay. I'm going to show you how this works right now.

Do the following short exercise.

Fill in the two blanks in this sentence as many times as you can. I call this my *key sentence*: "People who are shopping for _____ on eBay *might* also be interested (and possibly willing to pay for) instant *information* on _____."

I've just given you the keys to the kingdom.

Burn that sentence into your mind. Write it on a 3 × 5 card and pin it somewhere you can see it. That is a powerful concept. The words *might* and *information* are italicized for a reason.

As you think about filling in the blanks in that sentence, don't limit yourself to eBay, and don't just think about topics that interest you. Brainstorm for a minute. Think of your friends who have strange hobbies or unusual businesses in your community. Use your imagination to walk through a shopping mall and think about our key sentence, or surf eBay and see what is selling. Fill in the two blanks as many times as you can. Since nearly 400 million customers are shopping around on eBay with credit cards in hand, the possibilities are endless.

Each time you complete that key sentence you are generating new ideas for silent sales machines on eBay. Even if you know nothing about the product being sold, you can easily find experts with whom you can partner to create a great information product.

Once you have an informational topic in mind, don't make the mistake of thinking you must write a book. Your book could be as simple as interviewing an expert and having the conversation transcribed into a word processing document. Done.

(Continued)

I'm living proof that e-books sell on the Internet. I've sold around 200,000 myself. I have friends who are pulling in $10,000 to $15,000 every month on eBay selling e-books and information products. *Tip:* You can meet many of the most successful eBay sellers I know over at MySilentTeam.com. I encourage you to check that out—it will inspire you, I promise.

Let's say you already have an info product you've written or bought the resale rights to and now you are trying to market it on the Internet. The key sentence also works in reverse in that case.

I'll give you an example. I was once approached by a customer who was trying to market a computer tips book for home PC users. He was wondering how to market it on eBay. His key sentence was "People who might be interested (and possibly willing to pay for) instant information on PC tips are likely also shopping for _____." The obvious answer in his case is "computer components and computer supplies."

Rather than suggest he set up a big computer components business on eBay to drive new customers his way, I instead advised him to find someone who had such a business already established on eBay and partner with them. He did, and it worked!

The Internet runs on win-win-win propositions just like that example. Here are the three wins:

1. The *customer* wins because he gets a great free or inexpensive e-book containing PC tips with each order.
2. The *eBay seller* wins because without doing anything, he is adding value to the customer experience and, as a result, selling more.
3. The *owner* of the PC tips book wins because he's now selling his book or growing his mailing list or both.

I could go on for several pages about these concepts, but I can't do that here. If you would like more strategies and information, feel free to visit MySilentTeam.com and get my free newsletter. It's all about the creative Internet income strategies that I've used to grow an online empire.

Jim Cockrum has inspired tens of thousands of people with his creative yet down-to-earth style. He's sold millions of dollars of products and services and has helped others start successful eBay and online businesses since 2000. He earns his living from the Internet and he works full-time educating others on how to run successful Internet and eBay businesses. You can read more about his work at www.SilentSalesMachine.com.

Resource Page

Summary of topics discussed in this chapter:
- ☞ How to get started on eBay.
- ☞ Decide what to sell.
- ☞ Determine pricing.
- ☞ How to buy for resale on auction sites.
- ☞ How to promote your auction.
- ☞ Shipping methods.
- ☞ Time your auction.
- ☞ The path of the PowerSeller.
- ☞ Treat it like a real business.
- ☞ Learn about the bells and whistles.
- ☞ Go beyond eBay.

Our guest expert writes about using eBay to build a larger Internet business.

Go to www.YourInternetCashMachine.com and find a variety of resources related to auction sites, as well as interviews with our guest experts. Claim your free membership now!

A CLOSER LOOK AT AFFILIATE SALES SITES

As we stated earlier, an *affiliate* is a person who refers potential new buyers to a seller's site. Affiliate-specific sites are set up to provide an additional venue where people can come and buy from the merchants with whom the site owner is affiliated. Affiliate sites may be the single business model that has created the most wealth on the Internet. Many affiliate businesses are producing six- and seven-figure incomes for their owners. It has been estimated, however, that 10 percent of active affiliate sites are producing 90 percent of affiliate site income. This figure emphasizes the importance of following the action steps presented later in this book.

ADVANTAGES

Affiliate sites offer a number of advantages. In addition to being potentially very lucrative, affiliate sites can be up and generating income quickly. As is true of most Internet businesses, setup costs are low. An affiliate can sell almost any product imaginable, or any combination of products. When you find a niche that excites you, you can easily identify products in that niche for which you can become an affiliate. There are many thousands of affiliate programs available. You can be an affiliate for building materials. You can be an affiliate for shoes. You can be an affiliate for dental services, for legal insurance, for stock brokerages, or for credit cards.

Affiliates do not carry inventory and are not responsible for processing orders or shipping. You will not need a merchant account to be an affiliate. Because you will be selling other people's products, you do not need to incur the time and cost of producing products of your own. Sales experience is not necessary, and you need not develop your own marketing materials. The company you represent will provide you with everything you need to sell their products. If at any time one of the products you represent is not selling well, you can easily drop it and pick up another product. Your risk is minimal.

With an affiliate site, as with any Internet business, you control your income to an extraordinary degree. Your success depends on how well you are able to present your information, and how many people you can attract to come to your site and click through to the merchant for whom you're an affiliate. Finally, as an affiliate, you can live almost anywhere in the world.

MAKING MONEY AS AN AFFILIATE

The mechanics of affiliate sites are straightforward. When you sign on to a merchant's affiliate program, you are given links to place on your site or send out in your newsletter and e-mails. Visitors to your site click on the link and are transferred to the merchant's site. When your visitor makes a purchase from the merchant, or takes another specified action, your account is credited. Each affiliate link contains your specific identifier, and software on the merchant's site tracks your sales and the leads you generate.

Generally affiliates are paid one of three ways. The first is cost per action (CPA), such as compensation for lead generation. Imagine you are a wine aficionado and have a site devoted to wine. Your site might include information about French wines, California wines, Portuguese wines, Australian wines, and Texas wines. And, of course, you offer affiliate links there.

A visitor to your site may click on an affiliate link to get information about a tour of the Napa Valley for wine tastings and perhaps a stay at a bed and breakfast on a winery. The visitor is routed to the merchant's site and reads about the trip. He thinks, "Wow. I'd love to do that, but not this month." Still, he signs up for the merchant's newsletter. Now the merchant's site has generated a lead from your affiliate link, and if the merchant has a pay-per-action program, you have earned a commission.

The second way for affiliates to be paid is cost per click (CPC). In that case, you as an affiliate are paid every time a visitor clicks through your site to the merchant's site, regardless of whether that visitor takes additional action.

The third way affiliates are paid is cost per sale (CPS). Cost per sale is the most concrete operation and it is the biggest moneymaker for affiliates. Often it is the only type of payment offered by merchants. In this case, your visitor goes to your site about wine, finds the tour of the Napa Valley for wine tasting, pulls out his or her credit card, and says, "Yes, this is what I am doing this summer." And you, the affiliate, receive a percentage of the sale.

There are also some programs that pay on the basis of cost per impression (CPM). However, these programs are not usually profitable for the affiliate, as they are often associated with sweepstakes or efforts to collect e-mail addresses for future campaigns.

HOW TO SELECT MERCHANT PARTNERS

Once you have decided the theme of your affiliate site, the next step is to find merchants you would like to represent. One of the best ways to locate merchants is through an *affiliate network*. Affiliate networks are companies that provide affiliate programs for merchants and make these programs available for affiliate site owners. The network provides marketing materials, tracks statistics, and usually issues commission checks. Most networks pay affiliates one monthly check regardless of how many merchants you may represent.

As an affiliate, you may usually join an affiliate network at no cost. You submit an application that includes your contact information. Approval of your application may be immediate, or it may take up to a week or more. Once your application is accepted you can go through the affiliate network database and select the merchants you wish to represent.

Here are some affiliate networks you might find helpful:

☛ *www.Advertising.com.* Advertising.com represents over half of the top 100 online advertisers. Their affiliate programs have no minimum traffic requirement, and there is no cost to join. Applications are approved in two days. Checks are issued for monthly commissions of $25 and above.

☛ *www.AffiliateFuel.com.* Affiliate Fuel is another of the largest networks. To qualify as an affiliate through Affiliate Fuel, sites must receive at least 2,000 unique visitors daily, have professional design and good content, and receive 90 percent of their traffic from the United States and Canada. Applications take ten days for approval. Checks are issued for monthly commissions of $25 and above.

☛ *www.ClickBank.com.* ClickBank is an online distribution service for digital products such as e-books and audio and video products. ClickBank's network includes over 100,000 affiliates. You can set up an account and immediately begin offering products from ClickBank. Checks are mailed twice monthly, and are issued for affiliate commissions above $10 per payment period.

☛ *www.Clickxchange.com.* Clickxchange is known for its user-friendly statistical reporting system. Affiliates earn a lifetime 5 percent for affiliate referrals and a 50 percent fee on advertiser referrals. Checks are issued monthly.

☛ *www.ClixGalore.com.* ClixGalore represents 4,500 merchants and tens of thousands of affiliates. In addition to the usual marketing materials, ClixGalore offers affiliates the "Instant Website Builder" tool, which instantly generates promotional web pages for their merchants' products. Affiliates earn a lifetime 5 percent commission for all affiliate referrals. Monthly payments are made to affiliates for any earnings over $50.

☛ *www.cj.com.* Commission Junction's web site declares that its network is used by "more advertisers on Internet Retailer's Top 500 Guide to Retail Web Sites than the next two affiliate marketing providers combined." Affiliate applications are processed quickly. Payments are made monthly.

☛ *www.DarkBlue.com.* Dark Blue operates on a different model than most affiliate networks. Instead of taking a portion of payments by merchants to affiliates, Dark Blue makes its profit from a pop-under generated from each affiliate's web site as a visitor exits the site. Dark Blue provides an instantaneous application process for affiliates. Affiliates are paid monthly for any amount earned over $30.

☛ *www.iWhiz.com.* iWhiz states they have one of the highest-paying affiliate networks on the Internet. In order to qualify as an iWhiz affiliate, your site must receive a minimum of 5 million unique page views per month, or you must have a mailing list of at least 50,000 persons. Commissions are paid monthly, but the affiliate must have earned $500 in order to be paid.

☛ *www.LinkShare.com.* Link Share represents hundreds of major merchant companies and is among the most successful of the affiliate networks. Unlike many of these networks, LinkShare uses proprietary technology rather than cookies to track affiliate sales. LinkShare's affiliate contract specifies that merchants are responsible for paying all commissions to affiliates.

☛ *www.Performics.com.* Performics represents 300 merchants, including a number of large, well-recognized brands. Affilates are paid monthly for all sales in excess of $50.

☛ *www.PrimaryAds.com.* Primary Ads requires affiliate sites to have a minimum of 100 unique page views each month. Affiliates are paid monthly for any amount earned in excess of $25.

☛ *www.Search4Clicks.com.* Search4Clicks is an affiliate network representing hundreds of education-oriented merchants. Checks are issued monthly for amounts earned in excess of $50.

☛ *www.ShareaSale.com.* The Share a Sale network represents over 2,000 merchants in 38 categories. Affiliates are paid monthly for amounts earned in excess of $50.

After you have spent some time reviewing the affiliate networks, you may want to visit the following sites:

☛ *www.associateprograms.com.* This site, owned by successful affiliate marketer Allan Gardyne, features a directory of almost 10,000 companies with affiliate programs. There is also a collection of articles and resources, plus a forum for affiliates.

☛ *www.affiliatetip.com.* The Affiliate Tip site features a directory of affiliate programs, Shawn Collins' Affiliate Tip blog, and a variety of tools for affiliate marketers.

☞ *www.affiliateseeking.com*. Affiliate Seeking.com is a directory of over 1,700 merchant affiliate programs. It also includes a variety of articles useful to affiliate marketers.

The sites just listed will give you a place to start looking for merchants to represent. Google searches for "affiliate networks" and for "affiliate program directories" return a bonanza of sites useful to affiliate marketers. Also, many smaller merchants have affiliate programs they manage themselves. If you find a product you would like to represent, look for a link on the site marked "Affiliates," "Partners," or "Make money with us." If there is no affiliate program mentioned on the site, e-mail them and ask.

By now you have figured out there are perhaps millions of affiliate programs available to you as an Internet marketer. So how do you decide which company and which products to choose? Following are some questions you can ask:

☞ *Are the products appropriate to your site?* If you have a site about wine, you might sell cheese baskets, but it's not likely that you are going to be selling automobile seat covers. That's not why visitors are coming to your site.

☞ *Is the merchant's presentation professional?* Even if you are working with a small company, you want to know the merchant is businesslike. You want them to be organized and have a grasp on the whole process so that you can be sure the bookkeeping will be taken care of, you will get paid, and they will give you good information. And most of all, you want to protect your customers, because those customers are the lifeblood of your business.

☞ *Do you own and like the product?* If you are happily married and you decide to set up a site for dating services, chances are you are not going to try the product. But find out as much as you can about the merchant, because you're putting your personal reputation on the line when you represent a product.

☞ *Is the pricing fair?* You're not going to sell something if it is tremendously overpriced. People on the Internet may be discovering new markets and new industries, but assume your customers generally are fairly savvy. If the prices are fair and competitive, you are more likely to be successful with the products.

☞ *Is the customer service good?* It is very difficult for your customer to differentiate between you, the affiliate, and the merchant. If your customer buys something and has an unhappy experience with the customer service, they will complain to you as well as to the merchant.

☞ *What's the commission rate?* You would be amazed to discover the difference in commission rates, even in the same markets. Dating services are a great example. Commissions paid by dating sites vary hugely. Why would you represent somebody who only pays a small commission? Do your homework, look at all the programs, and find somebody who pays a big commission.

☞ *How long do the cookies last? Cookies* are the software that tracks what web sites are visited by a person's computer. So if someone comes to your wine site and clicks through to your merchant, the tour guide in Napa, that tour guide will know the customer is coming from your wine site and will identify them through cookies that get planted in the customer's computer. Cookies can last 30 days, they can last a year, or they can last forever. Of course, the person who is doing the buying can remove the cookies, but statistics show only about 10 percent of Internet users disable cookies on their computers. So, generally speaking, cookies are an effective way for affiliate software programs to track who referred the sale. A very important question to ask is, how long is your credit from that customer going to last?

☞ *Do you qualify for the merchant's program?* Some merchants require a certain level of traffic to your site every day. Is their agreement nonexclusive? Generally speaking, unless you have a really wonderful deal, you don't want to get into an exclusive agreement. You don't want to be limited to representing only one merchant in a particular industry. You want to be able to offer your customers a variety of services.

☞ *Is their agreement two-tier?* Some are and some are not. In a two-tier program, if a customer comes to your wine site, clicks through to the Napa excursion, and loves it, and she just happens to have a vacation web site and decides she might like to become an affiliate for the Napa folks, too, you will profit. She will be categorized as an affiliate under you, and you'll get part of her commission every month.

☞ *What are the payment terms?* Do they only pay you when you earn $1,000? Do they only pay you every three months? You don't really want to have to wait for your money. One of the reasons people love ClickBank is because they pay every two weeks, just like clockwork. You may get a check for $500, you may get a check for $40, but it keeps rolling in. We all like to get paid. It keeps us motivated. So find out what the payment terms are.

In surfing the Web, you have probably come across web sites that are just a collection of links to other products or sites. Although these are technically affiliate sites and undoubtedly generate some income, they are unlikely to be highly ranked by the search engines, and they will not be accepted into the affiliate programs of many merchants.

INCLUDE VALUABLE CONTENT

Remember the primary reason most people use the Internet? We discussed it in Select the Best Business Model for You. The answer is *information*. Content is king on the Internet. Sites with interesting, frequently updated content are favorites of the search engines, as you will learn in Part Two. More importantly, however, content attracts visitors to stay and read, to return again, and often to purchase. In terms of Internet marketing, on affiliate sales sites as in other types of business sites, content can be considered preselling. Following are some examples of affiliate sales sites that offer excellent content of great interest to their visitors.

E-Commerce Confidential (www.ecommerceconfidential.com) is a site owned by our friend Bill Hibbler. Bill has an excellent reputation as a knowledgeable Internet marketer, and he is respected for the integrity of his information. In this site, Bill offers no-holds-barred reviews of Internet marketing products, based on his firsthand experience with the products.

A number of products are listed for sale on Bill's site. Some of them, such as *The Rudl Report,* are products Bill wrote or produced himself. Many are products for which he is an affiliate. What makes Bill a strong advocate for his readers, and a really successful Internet marketer, is that he uses all of these products and carefully examines them. Before he recommends them to his readers, he makes sure that they give value.

Go to Mexico (http://www.go2mexico.com/) is aimed toward visitors who are thinking about traveling to Mexico but don't know a lot about the country. These visitors may have heard of Cancun and Cozumel and Mexico City, but most of Mexico is unknown to them. They are looking for guidance on possible destinations, safety issues, laws in Mexico, places to stay and eat, fishing guides, and a host of other topics. The site is packed with valuable content, and at first glance most visitors would not think of it as an affiliate sales site. But in fact, almost every link on the site is an affiliate link.

Earlier we mentioned dating sites. Sage Hearts (www.sage-hearts. com) is owned by Rosalind Gardner, an affiliate marketing expert who makes seven figures a year from her group of affiliate sites. Sage Hearts includes a blog and online dating news. Rosalind reviews different dating services. She reviews books and movies. She gives you ideas about where to go on dates. She has a section set up specifically for seniors. She has created a site with content that is interesting to people who are looking for a partner, looking to date, and are considering using the Internet to meet people. In doing so, she has created hundreds of opportunities to represent and endorse various merchants.

GOOGLE ADSENSE

AdSense is Google's affiliate advertising program, through which Google places ads on your web site, and pays you when visitors click through to the advertisers' sites. You are paid for each and every click, not for sales. The amount you are paid is based on the cost of the keywords (see below), as well as the time of day, month, and season.

The ads are written by the advertisers, who essentially buy traffic by bidding on keywords through Google's AdWords program. Keywords are the individual words or groups of words used by Google visitors to search the Internet. For example, someone looking for information on this book might search using the title as keywords: "Your Internet Cash Machine," or he might type in "Internet business" or "Vitale + Wheeler."

For example, Jillian's business uses Google's mail program, Google Apps. You may be familiar with gmail (www.gmail.com), a version of this program. Jillian recently went to her inbox and read an e-mail from a customer in Salt Lake City, Utah. As she glanced at the e-mail, she noticed on the right of the screen a row of ads targeted to Utah. One was directed toward Mormons (many Utah residents are Mormons), another was for a ski program in the Utah mountains, and a third was for a restaurant in Salt Lake City. This very specific targeting is a function of Google's superior relevance formula, which also provides the highly targeted search results that have made Google so popular with researchers.

AdSense ads are available in a number of different sizes and formats, including banners, buttons, towers, and rectangles. The ads may be comprised of either graphics or text. You may also adjust the colors of the background, border, text, and links in the ads. The AdSense system offers a URL filter that allows you to make sure you do not end up displaying your competitors' ads. Also, be aware Google considers it fraud for you to click through ads on your own site, and they have sophisticated tools to identify rule breakers.

Although you will see Internet sites filled with AdSense ads and no content, these sites are generally not profitable over the long term, for two reasons. First, as you have already heard from us, and as you will read in Get the Word Out when we discuss search engine optimization, content is highly prized by Google and the other search engines. Second, Google frequently changes its formulas. In fact, there's even a name for it: the Google dance. When Google dances, what was once profitable may suddenly become unprofitable, and the site owner must adjust. For any type of affiliate sales site, regardless of whether you include AdSense in the mix, your best strategy is to offer at least as much valuable content and information as you do advertising.

In this chapter, we have discussed information specific to affiliate sales sites. But, as we're sure you have noticed, many types of Internet businesses can benefit from a more limited use of the affiliate selling model. If you have decided your new Internet business will be an affiliate sales site, you will find all the information you need to get going in Part Two.

Resource Page

Summary of topics discussed in this chapter:
- ☛ Advantages of affiliate sites.
- ☛ How to make money as an affiliate.
- ☛ How to select your merchant partners.
- ☛ Include valuable content on your site.
- ☛ How to use Google AdSense.

Affiliate links are fairly easy to recognize, and affiliate link theft is a common problem for affiliate marketers. To read more about this problem, and to learn how to protect yourself, visit www.YourInternet CashMachine.com. Access interviews with our guest experts. Claim your free membership now!

MARKETING THROUGH SOCIAL NETWORKING SITES

MySpace, FaceBook, and the other social networking web sites have for several years been popular meeting places for teenagers and young adults. Gradually, however, businesspeople have begun to see the advantages of tapping into this fresh market. It began when bands and individual musicians built their own MySpace pages. Soon they were joined by artists and authors. In the past year, Internet business owners have been throwing their hats in the ring.

MySpace and the other social networking sites allow you to create your own page. Individuals who set up pages on these sites tend to talk about themselves and their own interests. But as you will see later in Make it Hypnotic!, the successful marketer puts aside his ego and talks about his visitors, and *their* interests and concerns. Treat your MySpace or other social networking site as a marketing page; observe and respect the conventions of MySpace, but never forget your purpose in being there.

At these sites you can search for people who share your interests and ask to be added to their "Friends" list. You can also create your own Friends list, which can number in the thousands. MySpace allows you to feature up to 24 of them on your page, with photos and links to their pages. There are also forums where you can post topics and send links to your friends.

In addition to the exposure and networking possibilities provided by the social network sites, the search engines accord them substantial relevance. We have invited guest expert Adam Ginsberg to give you valuable tips on using MySpace. He is writing specifically about building an eBay business, but we encourage you to think how you can use these techniques to build any type of Internet business.

GUEST EXPERT ARTICLE

USE MYSPACE TO BUILD YOUR eBAY BUSINESS

Adam Ginsberg

The Internet is changing, and eBay is changing, too. In today's competitive online environment, it's important to stay ahead of your competition.

To make money on eBay, you need to understand eBay fundamentals and basics. You've got to understand how to best utilize titles and descriptions. Having a powerful eBay template and "About Me" page will also add to your success.

Now here's a strategy you won't learn on eBay: Use MySpace to promote and grow your eBay business.

What is MySpace? It is the largest social networking site on the planet, with more than 200 million members. Actually, MySpace adds more than 200,000 new profiles daily. And the best part is that MySpace is free!

First, you'll want to set up a MySpace profile, which you can do at http://www.myspace.com. A good profile page is very important. eBay allows you to create a special page called the "About Me" page, where you can let people know more about you. A MySpace profile is like an advanced "About Me" page, without the restrictions that

(Continued)

eBay imposes on its user base. For example, it's not against MySpace policy, as it is on eBay, to promote your non-MySpace web site.

Second, you'll want to customize your MySpace page with your own pictures and videos. You might also want to use a customized MySpace layout to give your profile a personalized touch.

Next, you will need to add friends to your MySpace page. On MySpace you can add friends of any sociological demographic, from age to gender to income.

What is a MySpace friend? A friend on MySpace is like a name in a database. Friends, those who have accepted a "friend request," are people on MySpace to whom you can send email, post bulletins, and even place a comment on their MySpace page.

When using MySpace, you can search or browse other MySpace users. Once you've found someone with whom you would like to network, simply click on the "Add friends" button to send this person a friend request. When that user accepts your request, he or she becomes part of your MySpace friends list.

MySpace also includes a blog, or online journal, where you can let the world know about your latest eBay listings. Here you can include links to your eBay store or directly to specific eBay listings.

How often should you post a blog comment? At minimum once a week, and ideally about three times a week. On MySpace you can track the number of times your blog has been viewed. Over time, as you add friends, you'll see this number continue to increase.

MySpace was originally created for garage bands as a way to network with other bands, but this changed quickly, and now more than 70 percent of MySpace users are over the age of 25. In most cases, this is the ideal demographic to sell your eBay items to.

There's nothing like free publicity and promotion. Use MySpace to promote yourself, your web site, and your auctions. Include this information not only on your MySpace profile but using MySpace blogs and comments as well, and you'll see the traffic to your eBay listings skyrocket!

Adam Ginsberg is the author of the number one best-seller, How to Buy, Sell, and Profit on eBay *(Collins, 2005). He has been featured in* Fortune, Entrepreneur, *and* Kiplinger *magazines, and has appeared on* CNBC, ABC World News Tonight, *and the* Today Show. *For more information, visit www.AdamGinsberg.com.*

Sam Heyer is the perfect guest expert on social networking sites for a variety of reasons. First, he is a brilliant Internet marketer who, in a very short time, has built an impressive resume of accomplishments. Second, he and a partner are about to introduce TuYu, a brand new cutting-edge social networking site that promises to revolutionize that business model. Finally, he's only 21 years old—his generation started all the excitement—so he has the inside track on understanding social networking. While we're wrapping our minds around the whole concept, Sam is moving ahead and showing us the way.

GUEST EXPERT ARTICLE

A NEW MODEL OF SOCIAL NETWORKING

Sam Heyer

I want to give you a quick crash course on a powerful marketing concept that is revolutionizing business in this new technology age. The concept is *social proof*.

Social proof is a psychological phenomenon in which people see others behaving in a certain way and assume it to be an appropriate mode of behavior; or they see people they esteem approving of something, so they themselves will approve of it.

Wow—understanding this principle and how to use it effectively (and monetize it) is what separates the good from the great, and is the difference between making just enough money to get by and making more money than you can spend.

All of us experience this phenomenon on a day-to-day basis without really even thinking about it. On average, about 70 percent of what we talk about daily centers around products, services, and news. We talk with our friends about great products we've used, horrible service we've received, and newsworthy topics we've read in the paper (or watched on TV) about XYZ company.

(Continued)

The question I always get asked is, "Can this social proof be manipulated?" The answer is yes—but not in the way you would think.

If you manipulate this process to get people talking about something that is not true, the buzz will die out when people discover the truth—and, long story short, your reputation will be destroyed.

We tell people things in order to make conversation, to demonstrate our knowledge, and most importantly, to better their lives by having them do (or not do) something that we did. Your listeners trust you, and you are not going to jeopardize that trust by giving them wrong advice about something—and vice versa.

The key word here is *trust*.

And this is why social proof is so powerful. You are not doing the selling, but your customer is. It's nothing new, but the Internet has made it easier than ever for an evangelist to get news of your product out to the world. At the same time, if the product is poor, people can spread the word on its lack of quality.

Social proof has also opened the doors to a new type of business. Let me fast-forward to present time and the beauty of the Internet. MySpace has 200 million-plus users. YouTube is the fourth largest site online. This is social proof at its finest.

These sites are true Internet phenomena, but they are just the beginning. Within the next few years there is going to be a major change on the Internet. When you go to a web site you will no longer see a sales letter trying to get you to buy something. You will see a social networking site with 10,000 members who love this product, and offering what other customers feel are the pros and cons. There will soon be numerous social networking sites for every niche you can imagine, and the field will only continue to grow.

As a consumer, what goes through your mind when you see a huge number of customers on a company's site? "All those people can't be wrong, so I know I won't get scammed, and they wouldn't be here if it was a bad product." You immediately have a sense of trust in the company or person selling the product or service. Can you imagine what this could do to their sales?

Now think of this powerful concept specifically applied to *your* product or service. What would it mean for your business if you could have your customers on your site building your brand—and those same raving customers being the ones who do your selling for you?

For you as a marketer, the benefits of using the social networking model, expanded to leverage the power of social proof, can be truly mind boggling. You will build a stronger bond with your customers and prospects then you ever could before. You will see what they are talking about, what they liked about your product, and what they disliked, allowing you to continue to improve and be the best. And to top it off, you will have the same viral elements that have allowed MySpace and YouTube to grow faster than any other sites on the Web.

Everyone should have a social networking site tailored to their business. If you feel your business *can't* have a social networking site to reap the benefits just outlined, then you aren't thinking hard enough in terms of what your customers want.

At Long Run Marketing, we have clients ranging from the nano-technology industry to the male enhancement niche, and from real estate to a mortuary. (I never would have thought there would be a social networking site for when people pass away. I was wrong.) For every idea, passion, niche, and product out there, there is more than one person who is interested in it, and those people are interested in meeting others who share the same interest.

This is the true power of social proof and how you can easily apply it to your business, product, service, passion, or idea. Monetizing it is far easier than trying to line up advertisers for your site in the way MySpace does, because the next phase in social networking will include selling on the social networking site.

What you have read so far is the idea behind our company, TuYu, LLC. You can create your own, fully customizable, fully brandable social networking site at the click of a button (or have someone else do it). It has its own shopping cart and e-commerce solution so you can sell your own products, sell others' products, or charge a monthly fee for users to access your site.

Whether you're just getting started or have a Fortune 500 company, TuYu has the technology that will allow you to get the edge on your competition and connect with your customers and prospects in a way that has never before been possible.

(Continued)

This type of technology is the way of the future. Within several years, because of the power behind the technology, generic web sites will be obsolete. With TuYu, you can be part of the future of the Internet, right now. With TuYu, you can immediately propel your business far ahead of the competition.

To see for yourself what the power of TuYu technology can do for your business and your bottom line, go to www.tuyu.com and test-drive it today.

And the best part is, harnessing this technology for your business is extremely simple and won't cost you the millions of dollars that it has for other companies to create their own social networking sites.

Sam Heyer and partner Lee Raito co-founded TuYu, LLC, after successfully using social networking tactics with their marketing company, Long Run Marketing, Inc., to sell over $1 million of a client's product online early in 2006. They have since gone on to reap enormous profits month after month. Savvy Internet marketing observers believe TUYU will change social networking online forever. Learn more at www.tuyu.com.

Resource Page

Summary of topics discussed in this chapter:

This chapter focuses on the operation of social networking sites and how to use them to market your Internet business. Articles by our guest experts are "Use MySpace to Build Your eBay Business" and "A New Model of Social Networking."

Go to www.YourInternetCashMachine.com and find a variety of resources related to social networking sites, including interviews with our guest experts. Claim your free membership now!

CREATE YOUR OWN INFORMATION PRODUCTS

E arlier we pointed out that most people who use the Internet are looking for information. There is a lot of free information available on the World Wide Web and, as dedicated Web surfers ourselves, we love that! Still, researching any topic, even on the Internet, is time consuming and calls for skills many people simply don't have and are not interested in developing.

Consumers are more than willing to pay for information that is easy to find and easy to use. Also, Internet users, like consumers in the bricks-and-mortar world, are willing to pay for the expertise of others. As an Internet marketer, you can take advantage of that willingness by creating and selling information products that provide value to your customers.

WHAT IS AN INFORMATION PRODUCT?

Information products come in many forms. This book is one. You've purchased this book because it contains information you want to have, or perhaps it was purchased by your local library and you picked it off the shelf because of the information presented here.

Articles are information products. In Part Two we show you how to use articles to drive traffic to your web site, but you can put together compilations of articles on any subject of interest, and sell that compilation.

How-to manuals are much in demand. If you know how to install a garage door, you could write a report with instructions and helpful hints on installing garage doors, and sell it online. Any skill you possess can be put into a how-to manual and sold. Can you imagine the possibilities?

Written reports are information products. For example, many people approaching retirement age are considering moving to another part of the country, perhaps for a more comfortable climate or a lower cost of living. You could create a report that compares the advantages and disadvantages of living in different towns, cities, and states. If you attend an interesting conference on a specific subject, you could write a report summarizing the information presented, and sell it to people who might have wished to attend, but were unable.

Speaking of conferences, many people who plan and sponsor meetings and events arrange to have audio and video recordings made, which they then sell on the Internet as information products. Attendees at conferences can also ask presenters if they are willing to be interviewed, and sell the written, audio, or video interviews as information products.

In the chapter, "A Closer Look at Online Auctions," we mentioned creating software products. If you are a programmer, you can create a software product people will want and sell it as an information product. But even if you have no programming skills whatsoever, all you really need is a good idea. Think of a need people have, and imagine what kind of software product would fulfill that need. Then hire a software programmer to create the product. In the chapter, "Set Up Your Web Site," we talk about a number of inexpensive resources for contract work, including programming.

DETERMINING DEMAND

We have been encouraging you to create your business in a field you truly enjoy, and we stand by that. Before you invest time creating a product, however, determine whether there is a market for it. Find out if anyone will be interested in buying what you create.

To determine the demand for a product, use keyword research. You probably already know about keywords, even if you haven't been using the term. A keyword, in the vernacular of the Internet, is a word or string of words used in an Internet search. If you are visiting downtown

Chicago, and you get a yen for Chinese (sorry, that was too hard to resist), you may go to your favorite search engine and enter "best downtown Chicago Chinese restaurant." Within a moment, your restaurant options appear on the screen.

Whatever product a customer is searching for on the Internet, she enters a keyword that leads her to the appropriate web sites. There are online services that track the frequency of searches on keywords, and that data can help you determine your potential market. On our web site, www.YourInternetCashMachine.com, we provide a free tutorial on how to do keyword research.

DELIVERY

In the early days of the Internet, most information products were created in a physical form and shipped to the buyers. Today it is possible to make most products available for immediate download.

Downloadable products provide benefits to customers. They offer instant gratification, and they can be stored on the buyer's hard drive or MP3 player, rather than taking up space in an office or on a bookshelf. Downloadable products offer even greater benefit to you as an Internet marketer, because you have absolutely no expense for handling and shipping. Consequently, most Internet business owners who sell information products now prefer the downloadable format.

There is one notable exception. If you are selling an expensive and complex product, you must consider two issues. The first is *visibility*. The majority of buyers are still most accustomed to holding a product in their hands and reading from the printed page. If they spend a lot of money to buy a product, they may want to see it arrive at their front door. The second issue is *perceived value*. A box with a bound manual and some beautifully packaged DVD cases has a much greater perceived value than would the identical information delivered as a few downloadable files.

BENEFITS OF INFORMATION PRODUCTS

Information products are inexpensive to produce. In fact, if the information is already in your possession (whether in your head or in your desk drawer), the only cost may be your time.

Because of the low production cost, the profit margin on information products is very high. Even in the event you decide to produce and ship a physical product, the cost involved relative to the profit is extremely low.

Delivery of downloadable information products is easy to automate. When you have completed your product, simply upload it to a web page. You then create a sales page with a purchase link. When the purchase is complete, your buyer is directed to the download page.

In the chapter, "A Closer Look at Affiliate Sales Sites," we told you about ClickBank, an online distribution service for digital products such as e-books and audio and video recordings. When you sell your information products through ClickBank, you have the benefit of their extended sales force of over 100,000 affiliates. ClickBank is designed for products with a fairly low price point, generally under $100. Joe is the co-author of one of the best-selling e-books on ClickBank, *The 7 Day eBook*. Over the years, this one digital product has made a significant contribution to Joe's overall income. Another resource similar to ClickBank is Pay Dot Com (www.paydotcom.com).

Our next guest expert, Tim Knox, is a humorist and a highly successful Internet marketer. He has produced hundreds of information products.

GUEST EXPERT ARTICLE

WHAT'S THE BEST PRODUCT TO SELL ONLINE?

WHY, INFORMATION, OF COURSE

Tim Knox

I wish I had a dime for every time I've been asked, "Tim, what's the best product to sell online?" I also wish I had a dime for every blank stare I received when I answered, "That's simple: information." I'd have enough dimes to finance a Hawaiian vacation or two.

As more and more entrepreneurs move to the Internet seeking their fortunes (it is the new gold rush, after all), "What's the best product to sell online?" has become the number one business question of the decade.

The next question is usually, "Why Information?" Again, the answer is simple: because no other type of product is easier to create, faster to bring to market, easier to distribute, and always more profitable than hard goods.

Informational products come in many forms. An info product can be a digital book (*e-book* is the accepted term), a report or white paper, a piece of software, a web site, a newsletter, an audio or video, a tele-seminar, and so on.

Information products can also be nondigital items like spiral-bound manuals, stapled white papers, or CDs and DVDs. I prefer the digital variety myself, but millions of dollars have been made by sharp entrepreneurs selling information that is delivered to their customer's door.

Here are six reasons why information is the best product to sell online.

1. *Fast to create, fast to market.* Forget a product development cycle that is years in the making. Forget costly design and manufacturing processes. I have literally created info products in as little as two hours and had them generating revenue shortly thereafter. If you have an appealing topic and a computer, you have all the tools you need to create an info product that could sell in the millions.

2. *No inventory to stock.* Forget filling your garage with boxes of cheap watches and cases of mega vitamins that you will never sell. When you sell information there is no inventory to buy and stock. Your product is digital (I call it "selling electronic air") and requires no space in your garage, just a little space on your computer. One of my most successful info products is a 30kb e-book that requires almost no space at all.

3. *Low startup costs.* When you sell information you can literally create a product for next to nothing. If your product is an e-book the only investment required will be the time it takes to

(Continued)

put words to digital paper. If you become an affiliate marketer of someone else's info product your investment can be *zero*. You simply sign up to their affiliate program, get your affiliate link, and start the marketing process.

4. *You can automate the sales and delivery process.* Thanks to Internet technology, you can sell info products 24 hours a day, seven days a week, and never lift a finger. In fact, you don't even have to be awake or at home to make money with an info product. I know many successful information entrepreneurs who are getting rich working as little as an hour a day. They check the web site and their e-mail, then go play golf or hang with the kids for the rest of the day.

   You can completely automate the sales and delivery process so your web site does everything for you. An automated web site can give a potential customer your sales pitch, take the order, process the payment, deliver the product by e-mail—and even follow up in a few days to make sure the customer is satisfied, and offer to sell them additional products.

5. *You can offer immediate access or delivery.* Online consumers are an impatient lot. They want things *now!* These are people who stand in front of the microwave impatiently tapping their foot and frowning at their watch. Selling information is the best way to give your customers immediate satisfaction. As mentioned earlier, an automated web site can process the order and payment, then immediately e-mail the download link for the product to your customer.

6. *There's no shipping and handling.* One of the things I never liked about selling hard goods was the manual process of taking the order, running the credit card, placing the order with a dropshipper, or filling the order of my stock. I hated finding a box and packing peanuts, printing the label, taping it all up, and lugging it to the post office. Every minute I spent filling orders was time for which I was not being compensated; therefore, my profit shrank with every minute spent on shipping and handling.

   Informational products require no shipping and handling. Most are delivered by e-mail. In the time it takes you to click your mouse, you can deliver an info product.

What If You Don't Have Your Own Info Product to Sell?

Now we come to one of the most appealing aspects of selling information. If you don't have an info product, creating or finding one is much easier than you think. What follows are some of my favorite ways to come up with info products without having to do it all myself.

☞ *Sign on with an affiliate program and sell their products.* There are thousands of companies that sell informational products and most, if not all, have affiliate programs that you can sign on with. I am a huge fan of affiliate programs because you can literally get started in business in just minutes. Becoming an affiliate basically means you become a reseller of the company's products. You promote the product, you make the sale, the company delivers the product, and you earn a commission.

☞ *Partner with someone who can put your ideas into words.* People whine at me all the time, "Tim, it's easy for you to create ebooks. You're a writer. But I'm not a writer! That makes it hard for me!" I could not disagree more. Even if you can't write your name on a check, you can still create an information product using a ghost writer who will write the book for a fee, or find a writer who will co-author the book for no up-front cost.

One of the best ways to create an informational product is by co-authoring. If you are an expert on a topic, but not a writer, find a writer to co-author the project with you. You can hire them on an hourly basis or by the project. The idea—the subject matter—is much more important than the execution, so who actually writes the material becomes a moot point. In my opinion, expert knowledge is harder to come by than writing skills. I know many experts who can't write and many excellent writers who don't have the expert knowledge to create an informational product. This can be a match made in heaven.

☞ *Hire a ghost writer.* A ghost writer is someone you hire to write the product for you, but they do so anonymously. You get the credit for the work. You supply the expertise and guidance.

(*Continued*)

The ghost writer puts it in a coherent format for you. There is no shame in using a ghost writer. I know some brilliant people who are experts in their fields but couldn't write a parking ticket. You would probably be surprised to discover that many of the most popular nonfiction books have been ghost-written. You don't really believe all those pro athletes and Hollywood actresses can write 300-page books now, do you?

☞ *Publish a directory*. Can't think of a subject that you're qualified to write about? Try compiling a directory. A directory is nothing more than a listing of specialized information that you target-market to a particular segment of the buying public. For example, my company publishes a drop-ship and wholesale industry directory that is a listing of company names, addresses, phone numbers, and web site addresses. I simply have someone research the industry and compile their findings in a directory format, package it nicely, and sell it online for $27.

The key to creating a successful info product is this: the information must be worth far more than the price of the e-book itself. If you're charging $27 for your product, it must give the buyer many times that price in perceived value.

Here are a few more tips on creating a winning information product.

☞ *Narrow your niche*. Make sure you are targeting a highly defined niche audience. Don't try to sell to everyone. You can get a lot more money showing life insurance agents how to find more customers to buy big insurance policies than you can trying to sell a product on generic sales skills improvement.

☞ *Point out their pain*. Make sure your info product hits a painful problem that members of your target audience will do just about anything to solve. The more intense the pain, the more they're willing to pay to get rid of it.

☞ *Let them take the puppy home*. Give people a taste of what you offer in your info product by giving them a sample for free. Just like the wholesale clubs get you to buy tater tots in a 50-pound bag by giving you one to try, you can induce people to buy your information by letting them read the first chapter or listen to the first few minutes of an audio.

☞ *Keep them entertained*. People hate to be bored. Increase the power of your product by adding humor, drama, and other entertainment elements that make them want more and more. This will not only help with future sales to satisfied customers, it will also keep your refunds down and increase word-of-mouth advertising.

☞ *Make it evergreen*. Don't make the mistake of creating a product that hits a fad or a fleeting market. Create info products that can be updated with very little effort. This allows you to create a product once and keep the sales rolling in for years to come!

Tim Knox is a newspaper columnist, radio host, Internet marketer, and the author of Everything I Know About Business, I Learned From My Mama. *His web site is www.TimKnox.com.*

Our next guest expert, Nerissa Oden, is a former Hollywood film editor and the creator of Video Codemaker. She is an advocate of free programs for video users, and an expert on what programs are available. We've asked her for ideas on creating video information products.

GUEST EXPERT ARTICLE

HOW TO MAKE AND SELL A VIDEO PRODUCT AT ZERO COST

Nerissa Oden

Every time I do a teleseminar, teleconference, or hold a workshop, I get overwhelmed with gratitude from strangers. Many had no idea that video-making software already existed on their computer. In one teleseminar a woman confessed that she had just bought a Mac because she thought PC computers couldn't edit videos. Other people

(Continued)

often chime in or e-mail me later saying that they had made their first video and posted it online before the call was over. That's the kind of reaction I hope you will have after reading this section.

In the past, professional video-making required equipment that was bulky, expensive, and lower quality. People didn't have access to cheap, high-quality camcorders and free video-making software until the late 1990s. And then things got *really* cheap and easy by the year 2003.

Before the late 1990s few people could afford to make professional videos. Most video projects before that time were produced by corporate entertainment, corporate business, the independently wealthy, and people who ran up their credit cards. And because I grew up living below the poverty line I was acutely aware that society's *video voice* (television and films) was limited to a wealthy few.

But no longer! Today, anyone can make a video with free video resources. Camcorders and web cams aren't even needed because you can make a video by importing photographs into video making software. You can even make video tutorials by capturing what's on your computer screen with free video-making software, CamStudio.

Getting Ready

Creating a video is your effort to communicate visually. When you create a video you will be trying to *recreate a language* that you've always understood in the past, but have never communicated. Think about that for a minute.

When I was a freelance video editor, I accepted jobs editing videos that were low-quality and incomplete, because I knew I could turn that video footage into something beautiful that communicated effectively. But many of my peers would only work jobs that involved video shot by a true professional cameraperson.

Now, why did I just tell you that? Because it's important to understand that when you operate a video camera you are in a *limited communication role*. You can do your best to capture every action, reaction, sound bite and more. You may even try to recreate a scene, a mood, or a light effect. Yet you are limited by time and chance, and many of us still end up with low-quality, incomplete video. But when you create videos with software, you are in a *very active communication role* because your options for how you can change and improve video and sound just skyrocketed.

Here are three free software programs for creating videos:

1. Movie Maker is included on Windows XP and Vista. Movie Maker can capture video from tape-based camcorders and web cams. It can also import video, audio, and picture files from hard drives, still cameras, and digital video cameras. Movie Maker is a simple but effective video editing software. Movie Maker video tutorials can be viewed at http://www.windowsmoviemakers .net/Tutorials/. You can learn more about Movie Maker and Windows XP at http://www.microsoft.com/windowsxp/downloads/updates/moviemaker2.mspx. And you can learn more about Movie Maker and Windows Vista at http://www.microsoft.com/windows/products/windowsvista/features/details/moviemaker.mspx.

2. iMovie is another simple but effective video editing software, located on Macintosh computers. Like Movie Maker, iMovie can capture video from tape-based camcorders and web cams. It can also import video, audio, and picture files from hard drives, still cameras, and digital video cameras. iMovie video tutorials can be viewed at http://www.apple.com/ilife/tutorials/imovie/. You can learn more about iMovie at http://www.apple.com/support/imovie/.

3. CamStudio is an open source, free video-making software. CamStudio is able to record all screen and audio activity on your computer in a variety of ways—full screen, dedicated area, dedicated window. It creates industry-standard AVI video files and Flash video files. It has no video editing features—just a start and stop button. Learn more about CamStudio at http://camstudio.org/.

Creating videos is easy and can be done for free. Making them communicate everything you want is a little harder. Here are a few questions you may ask yourself during the creative process:

☞ Which photo communicates the best?
☞ How long will a customer watch this clip and not get bored?
☞ Should I keep the audio? Add music?

(Continued)

☛   Will adding this effect to my video clip communicate better
or worse?
☛   Should I add text information to this video clip for clarity?
☛   Would narration help or hurt?

Making Your Video

After you've made all the creative decisions and the creative process
is complete, your video now exists as *project file*. A project file is part
of your video-editing software and can only operate and exist on
your computer. In general, a project file is a very small file that
keeps track of the creative decisions you made and references all
the media on your computer that you used in your video project.

Now, you must make a deliverable product from your video
project. This process is done within your video-making software. Common software terms for this process are *burn, export, output,* and *make.*

Video products are commonly made into one of these three
formats:

1. Video DVD disc.
2. Video file download.
3. Pay-per-view (PPV) streaming video.

Video DVD Disc

Turning your video project into a video disc is commonly called
burning. Video DVD burning software is included on Windows Vista
and Macintosh computers. Windows XP users can download Video
DVD Maker free at www.videodvdmaker.com.

Video DVD discs are physical products that cost you $0 when
you sell them through a third-party Internet company. Internet
companies www.Lulu.com and www.CreateSpace.com require you
to create an account with them. Then they provide you with an
e-store, accept customer payments, duplicate and package your
DVD, ship it, and handle returns and other customer questions.
Accounts are free, simple to set up, and you can add more DVD

products over time. To start working with either of these companies, simply follow these steps:

1. Sign up for your free account.
2. Upload (or mail) your video files and package artwork.
3. Write your description and set your price.
4. Promote your DVD.
5. Deposit your checks when they arrive.

Note: CreateSpace wasn't always free but has been offering a $0 setup fee for several months now. CreateSpace will also list your video DVD on Amazon.com at no cost if you want.

Video File Download

A video file is a copy of your video project rendered into just one file. Video-making software will typically make three or more different video file formats. The most common formats your software will make are AVI, MPG, and a Web-friendly format like WMV, MOV, or SWF. These files are considered friendly because they are smaller in size, which makes for faster download and play times. Movie Maker makes WMV files, iMovie makes MOV files, and CamStudio makes SWF files.

Tip: To locate free video encoder software to turn AVI and MPG files into desirable Web-friendly files, just visit www.FreeMediaGuide.com.

Video files sold as a downloadable file costs you nothing when you sell them through a third party internet company, such as www.Lulu.com and www.CustomFlix.com. To work with either company, follow the same steps listed previously concerning video DVD discs. CustomFlix can also set up your your video download with "Unboxed" on Amazon.com at zero cost, if you want.

If you own and maintain a web site, you can sell downloadable video files from it. One way to do this is to create a free publisher's account with www.Clickbank.com.

Need help posting a video in a web page? How do you want your video file to appear? In a large video player? A small player? As a text link? Or as an image link? Use www.FreeVideoCoding.com

(Continued)

to make your video file appear just as you want on your web pages.

Pay-per-View Streaming Video

Streaming video files can only be viewed, not downloaded or saved. This type of video product isn't named pay-*per*-view for nothing. Pay-per-view streaming video requires specialized software and equipment.

How does one sell a PPV video? Google Video (www.video.google.com) offers free video hosting accounts for public and private videos. Account holders with more than 1,000 videos to upload have the option to sell their videos as PPV. Google Video charges about 30 percent of the PPV sales as their fee for this service. Customers are also offered the option to pay for a download of your video. To offer your video as a PPV video today, most likely you will need to pay money up front to a video-hosting company that offers PPV as a feature. For example, www.vmdirect.com is a video-hosting company that is close to adding a PPV option to all the other specialized features that are included in their $49/month affiliate accounts.

For those who can afford a higher fee, I would suggest www.vividas.com and www.akamai.com. Both companies cater to small businesses and large corporations, and they have both been delivering PPV videos for their clients for years.

If you own and maintain a web site, you can sell PPV video from it. You will need the following key features:

☛ A web host that offers streaming media web servers.
☛ Software that creates streaming video files.
☛ The ability to sell passwords that stop working after 24 or 48 hours.
☛ The ability to encrypt video file URLs from tech-savvy viewers (encrypted links can also be set up to stop working after 24 or 48 hours).

For help in setting up your streaming video for sale, consult your web master and web host. You can also hire a tech savvy contractor at www.rentacoder.com.

Are you jumping up and down with joy now that you've read this section? Every day I am grateful that you can make better videos than I could when studying video and film in college—and you can make and sell them at zero cost. What a wonderful time to be alive!

Nerissa Oden is an author of books and software with 12 years experience in video and film postproduction. She became a Web entrepreneur in 2002 and continues to write and develop video resources. Her main website is www.TheVideoQueen .com. Also check out www.FreeVideoCoding.com, www.VideoCamera Projects.com, www.VideoCodeMaker.com, www.FreeMediaGuide.com, www.FreeVideoEditing .com, and http://www.thevideoqueen.com/marketingthesecret.html.

Resource Page

Summary of topics discussed in this chapter:
☛ Explanation of types of information products.
☛ Modes of delivery for info products.
☛ Benefits of information products.

This chapter also includes guest experts Tim Knox on information products, and Nerissa Oden on creating video products at zero cost.

Go to www.YourInternetCashMachine.com and find a variety of resources related to information products, as well as interviews with our guest experts. Claim your free membership now!

PART TWO

The Action Steps

Whatever business model you have selected for your Internet cash machine, there is a sequence of very concrete action steps you must take to make your business profitable. A common problem among new Internet business owners (and those of us who are experienced fall prey to this, as well) is *information overload*. There are so many products available and so many new techniques, all promising to show you how to make more money, that it is difficult to sift through them all and decide which to implement. The answer, we have found, is to put most of that information aside and simply concentrate on those steps you must take to get started, utilizing only those activities and tools that have proven value to your business.

So we encourage you, if you have bought information marketing products, to put them into a file and forget them for the time being. Right now, narrow your focus, and visualize in front of you a lighted path. Along the path are these critical action steps. Do the first, then move on to the second. Complete it and move on to the third, and so on. When you have traveled as far as you can see, and have completed all the action steps, you will have a business that is making money. Then go back and repeat the steps, and make even more money.

When you have a stable, profitable business, you can experiment with new ideas. We admire creativity, and there are many brilliant, inventive Internet marketers who are constantly generating new ideas. You may be one of them! But in the meantime, we promise you: *The action steps work.*

SET UP YOUR WEB SITE

EQUIP YOURSELF

Here is one of the most delightful aspects of starting an Internet business. You need very little equipment. You must have a computer, of course. Because technology changes so rapidly, we recommend you own a computer that is less than two years old. However, if yours is older but still functional, you can begin with that.

Although we have friends and family members who are Apple computer fanatics, and we love the creativity and flexibility enjoyed by Mac users, you will find that many of the programs useful to you as an Internet marketer are only compatible with a PC (a personal computer with a Windows operating system). Be sure you have installed a Windows 98 or newer system.

You really must have high-speed Internet. We actually started our businesses with dial-up service, but once we upgraded to high-speed, there was no going back. Today much of your business will involve audio and video files, which are simply time prohibitive to download with dial-up.

A printer is useful. Even though we do almost everything electronically, including filing, sometimes you really need paper. A scanner is helpful, although not necessary. Other optional equipment, but very useful to have, are a webcam or other video camera, and a digital camera.

GET YOUR PIECE OF INTERNET
REAL ESTATE

Remember that old expression from real estate? A real property is valuable because of "location, location, location." On the Internet, a piece of real estate is called a URL, which stands for uniform resource locator. Technically, the correct term is uniform resource *identifier*, the identifier for each web site that makes the World Wide Web possible. Another name for the URL is the *domain name*.

A URL, or domain name, is both the name of a web site and its address. For example, the URL of the web site associated with this book is www.YourInternetCashMachine.com. At least in the South, where we both live, *URL* is colloquially pronounced "Earl," as in "Say, Bubba, did you buy that URL?"

Your first step is to decide upon, and purchase, the URL for your new Internet business. Selecting the best URL is very important; in doing so, you will secure your own valuable piece of Internet real estate.

A URL consists of the introductory "www" for World Wide Web, the domain name you choose, and an extension. Among the available extensions are *.com, .org, .net, .gov,* and the country extensions such as *.ca* (Canada), *.uk* (United Kingdom), *.au* (Australia), and others. Among the newest extensions available are *.ws* and *.name*.

The most popular extension remains .com (pronounced "dot com"), because in practical terms, it is the default extension in most people's minds. So when potential visitors look for your site, they are most likely to enter a .com extension. If at all practical, we recommend you use a .com extension. However, so many .com names have now been claimed that new web site owners are expanding their horizons. For example, our friend Mark Joyner now uses the site www .MarkJoyner.name. The .org extension is usually used by nonprofit organizations, and .gov is reserved for government-related web sites in the United States.

Later in this chapter we offer our recommendations about where to buy your URL, and much more. First, however, we invite you to read our next guest expert article, by Marcia Yudkin. Marcia is famous among Internet marketers for selecting dynamite business and product names.

GUEST EXPERT ARTICLE

PROFITABLY NAMING YOUR NEW INTERNET BUSINESS

Marcia Yudkin

When you've got a great idea for an online business, your next step is a crucial one. You need an address for it that fits the idea and can easily be remembered and typed. You need a great domain name.

People often botch this step out of haste or frustration. Depending on the subject matter of your new business, you can try brilliant name after clever name, only to discover that someone has already reserved them. Or you come up with a halfway decent name that seems like it will do, and you grab it and forge right ahead, heedless of its weaknesses.

Use These Criteria for Screening Domain Names

Don't settle for a domain name with outsized disadvantages. Get off to your best possible start by using these guidelines.

A Good Domain Name Is Pronounceable

That is, someone who sees it written down can say it out loud. Imagine someone on the phone, calling a friend, "Hey, you've got to check out this cool web site I discovered! It's . . ." Just about anything with hyphens can't pass this test. Something with two or more hyphens flunks the test. When trying to convey a double-hyphenated domain name over the phone, you'll have to spell it at least three times and still the chances are not good that the other person will get it right.

Make sure you also test the domain name without any capital letters. When I heard an ad on TV for www.NoMoreAllNighters. com, I smiled, thinking it was a winner. However, when someone sent me a link to the web site in this form: nomoreallnighters.com

(Continued)

(which is how it would appear in many browsers), I read it as
NomoReallNighters.com and was totally baffled. Likewise, for years
I thought a Vermont friend's domain name was the very puzzling
www.MaDriver.com rather than MadRiver.com.

A Good Domain Name Is Spellable

Possible trouble spots include doubled letters of two sorts. First,
last-name domains like PassarettiPhotography.com create problems
because people won't remember whether there are one or two s's,
r's, and t's. My friend Denise Passaretti therefore sprang for the
domain name www.PhotosbyDenise.com.

Second, combinations of words with the same letter repeated at the
end of one word and the beginning of the next trip up lots of people.
For example, when turned into a domain name, would The Energy Spot
be www.theenergyspot.com or www.thenergyspot.com? People won't be
sure. Of course, in this instance and the preceding one, you could buy
up all the possible misspellings and redirect them to the spelling you
intend to use, but why not save yourself that hassle if you can?

A Good Domain Name Is Memorable

As I write this article, the domain www.zyzzyg.com is available, which is
really rare for a name using only six letters. I don't recommend using it,
though, because no one will be able to remember it. There isn't any hook
there for it to stick in the mind because it looks like a string of nonsense.

There are less obvious ways to confuse the memory. A client of
my naming company commissioned a new domain name because
with his existing one, people couldn't remember whether it was,
let's say, www.MyFastCashFactory.com or www.YourFastCashFactory
.com—one of which was a competitor.

How to Come Up With Domain Names That Aren't Taken

Most people do not use the following naming tactics, so you're
much more likely to find a domain name you can reserve by brain-
storming along these lines:

☞ *Focus on results.* What is the outcome or end result that people want to have from buying a certain product or service? How do they feel when they have finished the transaction? My own company name, Named At Last (www.NamedatLast.com), falls into this category.

☞ *Look for puns.* Make a list of relevant keywords, say each out loud, and play around with the sounds. Puns are much less likely than other kinds of names to have been registered because their component parts are not actual words. For instance, the name Sitesfaction, for a web design company, was a finalist in our first naming contest—and an available domain at that time despite tens of thousands of web design firms in the English-speaking world.

☞ *Think slang.* Let your imagination and memory fly around for pleasing-to-the-ear expressions. As of today, the domain www. BoyOhBoyToys.com for an online toy store is unregistered, as is a domain for its sister store, www.AttaGirlToys.com.

☞ *Go symbolic.* Suppose you're an expert on the horror genre and want to start a paid online community for horror fans. www .Horrorific.com, www.HorrorGate.com, and www.HorrorNet .com are all taken, but when I first made this list of clips, the less obvious and more vivid www.FrightOwl.com was not.

☞ *Vary real words.* "Google's name is a play on the word *googol*, which refers to the number 1 followed by one hundred zeroes," says the Press Center of the world's most successful search engine. "The word was coined by the nine-year-old nephew of mathematician Edward Kasner," it continues—providing another hint for creative naming: consult a kid.

Marketing guru Marcia Yudkin is the author of 6 Steps to Free Publicity and ten other books hailed for their outstanding creativity. Find out more about her naming company, Named At Last, which brainstorms new company names, new product names, tag lines, and more for cost-conscious organizations, at http://www.NamedatLast.com.

Once you have chosen your web site name, the next step is to purchase your URL. There are a number of companies selling URLs, and the cost varies widely. Some of those companies also offer web hosting, while others do not. For convenience as well as cost, we suggest you select your web host and obtain your URL through them. The company we recommend offers free domain names to their customers.

FIND THE BEST WEB HOST

Finding a reliable web hosting company is critical to your business, and your life will be simpler if you make a good choice from the beginning. If you are not pleased with your initial web host and need to make a change, that's a hassle. It takes approximately 48 hours to transfer a site from one server to another, and during that time your customers will be unable to access your site. Who knows how much business you may lose during that period?

Here are some of the most important considerations in choosing a web host. First, what is the capacity of their servers? Will their equipment be able to accommodate your business as it grows and needs increased bandwidth? What is their guaranteed percentage of uptime? If their servers are down, your web site is down, and even 1 percent downtime is too much. Do they promise secure routine backups and state-of-the-art virus protection?

Customer service is another high-priority consideration. Choose a company that offers service 24 hours a day, seven days a week. Live chat capability is useful, but when we are having a problem, we like to be able to talk to a real person on the telephone, even if it is the middle of the night.

Does the company provide you with an administrative interface that is easy to use? Does the plan accommodate an unlimited number of domains and e-mail accounts? Will your site be able to have a forum for your visitors to communicate with each other? You probably won't need that initially, but you may want to include a bulletin board function of some kind down the road. Will you be able to use a WordPress blog? (More about WordPress in Get the Word Out.)

Will you have access to a web site building tool? And, since there is a learning curve for even the simplest system, does the company provide easy-to-understand tutorials? Finally, is the price reasonable? There is quite an astounding variation in prices for web hosting.

The company Jillian uses to host her sites meets all the criteria we have mentioned. You can get details about this company and its services, and create your own account, at www.CashMachineDomains .com. This web host been around since 1996, and is very highly rated. They guarantee 99.9 percent uptime. Their high-performance Xeon servers and secure routine backups ensure total reliability, and they offer round-the-clock customer service by live chat and by telephone. Their hosting package is an excellent value at $5.95 a month (at the time of this writing, they are offering a discount of $4.95, but we're not sure how long that will last). The package includes a huge amount of disk space, a very high monthly transfer allowance, hosting for an unlimited number of domains and e-mail accounts, and the capability of installing forums and databases, as well as WordPress. They offer a web site building tool, an easy to understand administrative control panel, and excellent tutorials. They also offer a free domain name for life to their customers.

SET UP YOUR INFRASTRUCTURE

Once you have made arrangements for hosting, the next step is to set up your business infrastructure. Following are the basic components you need to get started.

Payment System

You must have a way to accept payments from your customers. That includes a shopping cart and a merchant account. A merchant account simply allows you to accept credit card payments over the Internet.

Your shopping cart must integrate with your merchant account, and preferably with PayPal as well. The system must have a secure server, both so that your customers can safely transmit sensitive data, and to protect you from liability. Also, your payment system should include the capability for your customers to purchase and download e-books and other digital products. Even if you do not plan to offer digital downloads now, you may in the future.

Autoresponders

An autoresponder is software that allows subscribers to sign up for your mailing lists, and it can be programmed to automatically send out prewritten e-mail messages. You may have used a simple autoresponder at work to let people know you would be on vacation on certain dates. As an Internet marketer, you will use your autoresponder service to collect names of visitors and customers and thus build your list, and to send out e-mail communications to your list(s). Your autoresponder software should include a *wizard* you can use to generate sign-up forms for your subscribers, as well as other forms for your web site.

You can design your sign-up box to collect only e-mail address information, or you can expand it to collect a visitor's first (or first and last) name, address, and/or phone number. Of course, take into consideration the reluctance on the part of most people to offer personal information. You will get the best response by asking for the least information.

Why would your visitors decide to give you their e-mail address? That's where the ethical bribe comes into play. Offer your visitors something of value, for free, if they will subscribe to your list. A report makes a good incentive. For example, visitors to Jillian's site, www.GrantMeRich.com, can sign up for her free grant tips. Chances are, if your visitor is really interested in your topic, he will consider this a fair trade.

Once your visitor has subscribed to your mailing list, your automated system will immediately begin sending him a preprogrammed series of e-mails, each containing one segment of the report. You can also include him when you send out regular broadcast e-mails. We discuss those in greater detail in the chapter, "Get the Word Out."

Most marketers maintain several lists of subscribers, according to their interests and their status. For example, you might have a list of readers who have not yet made a purchase from you. Then you may have another list of customers who have purchased items under $100, and a third list of buyers of more expensive products. You may have separate lists for buyers of separate products, particularly if they are unrelated. For example, Jillian has one list of subscribers who are interested in grants, one list of those interested in real estate, a third list for Internet business, and a fourth list for subscribers interested in the spiritual principles of success. She even has a sign-up form configured so new subscribers can choose which list they would like to join. You can view this sign-up sheet at www.GrantMeRich.com/nl.htm.

The autoresponder can be set up for single opt-in or double opt-in subscribers. Single opt-in subscribers are added to the list upon request, either their request or the request of the list owner. Double opt-in subscribers first receive a confirmation e-mail, to which they must reply, or which contains a link they can click, in order to be added to the list.

There are two schools of thought among Internet marketers regarding the opt-in process. Single opt-in builds a mailing list much faster and more efficiently, since statistics show approximately one-fifth to one-third of subscribers never complete the double opt-in process. However, double opt-in provides the list owner with greater protection in the case of spam complaints. The best autoresponder services will also handle any spam complaints you receive and will negotiate on your behalf with Internet service providers (ISPs) such as AOL, MSN, Yahoo!, Earthlink, and others. At the bottom of every message from you should appear a link the reader may use to unsubscribe.

Affiliate Program

If you have an existing business, or if you plan to manufacture, import, or create new products, including information products of any kind, you will want affiliate program software. This software makes it possible for you to enroll affiliates, track their sales, and compute payment to them. You should be able to sign up an unlimited number of affiliates, create and manage multiple affiliate programs, and pay your affiliates either by check or through PayPal. The software should include the capability for you to associate different products with different affiliate programs and to vary individual commission rates. You should be able to provide your affiliates with a variety of marketing tools.

Each of the services just discussed (payment system, autoresponder, and affiliate program) can be purchased separately, although that is quite expensive and unwieldy. At the present time, there is only one service available that provides an integrated solution for Internet businesses. This service will provide you with a payment system that is compatible with merchant accounts and PayPal, and will also provide you with a merchant account if you need one. It provides unlimited autoresponders and an excellent affiliate program. What makes this service so useful to us as marketers is the seamless integration it provides. When readers come to your site and make a purchase, and pay for it, they can immediately download the product if it is digital (or if not, you'll be immediately notified of the purchase). Then the customer's name is added to the appropriate mailing list so you can continue to contact them and offer them future opportunities. To read more about this service and set up an account, visit www.CashMachineCart.com.

DESIGN YOUR WEB SITE

Now it's time to actually plan your web site. This is a lot of fun. Whether or not you are an artistic type, you probably already have some pictures in your mind of your ideal site. After all, you have years of experience visiting and viewing web sites of all kinds. We recommend you take at least a few days to visit lots of different sites, make conscious observations on their appearance, and take notes about what you like and don't like.

The colors used in a web site have a strong psychological impact on your visitors. Among graphic designers and advertising experts, the combination of black, white, and red is believed to telegraph an appearance of authority, business acumen, and trustworthiness. Once you begin to look, you will notice that many web sites of big companies employ that combination. A similar effect is achieved with navy or royal blue and white, with red accents.

Our subconscious minds associate various qualities and internal states with each color. Green connotes wealth and growth. Yellow is often associated with intelligence, and it also reminds of us spring and sunshine. Orange provides a buzz of energy. Blue is the color of healing and tranquility. Red represents action. Pink reminds us of love and harmony. Purple represents luxury and wealth.

Your web site must convey an atmosphere of professionalism. After all, you are asking your visitors to pay money for your products or services, so it is important you communicate a sense of serious purpose and a businesslike attitude. A person landing on your home page will be inclined to do business with you based on the level of trust and confidence instilled by that first impression of your site.

Still, one of the most interesting paradoxes of Internet business is that, although the World Wide Web reaches every continent on planet Earth, the Internet is an intensely personal medium. Even though your web site will be accessible to millions of visitors from all over the world, people whom you would likely never otherwise encounter, those visitors are interested in making a personal connection with you.

The most successful web sites communicate a strong sense of identity. This may be a corporate identity, but in most cases it will be an individual personal identity. You can choose to cloak your identity behind a corporate veil, but our experience has shown you will be most successful if you allow people to get to know you. We have both met many wonderful people, and even made some close friends, among our visitors and customers. There are many more whom we will never meet, but who have honored us with their trust, simply because we have let them come to know who we are as individuals. In practical terms, that means we include our photographs on our sites, and we share selected personal information regarding our philosophies and activities. We keep our readers up-to-date on the important events of our lives and give them a behind-the-scenes glimpse as we travel, speak, and network with associates.

We do encourage you to strike a balance here. Take reasonable precautions to keep your private life private. Use a business address. Even though you may work out of your home, rent a virtual office to use as your business address. Every modest-size town or city has a store where you can rent a postal box and get a physical address. We suggest you not display photographs of your children or publish their names and ages. We make these recommendations out of a general sense of caution, recognizing there are some unbalanced people in the world. We believe people are generally good, however, and we have tens of thousands of readers who have enriched our lives as well as our bank accounts.

Unless your business is an opinion site that highlights your political or religious point of view, we recommend you stay mute on those topics. Your grandmother was on to something when she instructed you to avoid dinner table conversation about politics and religion, and today that is truer than ever. It is unfortunate we can't all share our various points of view without fear of censure and with mutual understanding, but in our current rabid talk radio culture, there is no point alienating potential customers.

Politics and religion aside, however, let your individuality shine through on your site, particularly in your blog (we say more about blogs in Get the Word Out). Inject your own unique sense of humor and personality. Write about the things that interest you, and don't be afraid to be a little controversial. After all, pablum isn't very tasty, and that goes for intellectual pablum, as well. Give your readers a reason to come back for more of your personal wit and wisdom. If your friends consider you quirky and unique in some way, make sure your readers see that side of you, too.

A good way to begin the actual design of your site is to do a layout on paper. The heart of your site will be your *home page*, also called your *index page*. When your visitor arrives at your site, your business message should be the first thing he sees. There should be no doubt as to what kind of services and products you offer. Most sites also have an "About Us" or similar page, product catalog pages, and pages devoted to content of interest to your visitors.

Include only those pages that are relevant to your topic. Keep your design clean and simple, with plenty of white space. Don't confuse your visitor with a multitude of choices. Make it easy for him to find his way to access content, and to buy. Limit your use of exotic design elements such as Flash technology. You want your site to be attractive, but you are not entering an art contest. Keep your attention, and your visitor's attention, on your message. Studies show the average web site visitor will spend only a few seconds waiting for a site to load, so limit your graphic, audio, and video elements to those that will display almost immediately.

Ease of navigation must be one of your primary considerations. When a visitor arrives on your home page, she should be able to immediately understand the layout of the site and find links to all the other pages. We devote a later section entirely to search engine optimization, but it is important to know a few facts from the beginning. Your site will be more easily found and indexed by the search engines if you put your links on the right-hand side of the site. The information you want referenced in the search engines should be at the top of the page. As much as possible, link all your pages to each other, except in the case of your product sales pages. From a sales page, your visitor should have no obvious options other than to click on "Buy Now"!

Unless yours is an affiliate sales site, do not include links to other sites. That's like welcoming a cherished guest into your home and immediately showing him to the back door. It's hard enough to keep your visitor's concentration focused on your site. Never invite him to leave! If you sell products on an affiliate basis as a limited part of your business, keep those affiliate links on the product sales page. If for some reason you feel you must provide links to other sites, keep them together on a separate page.

Be sure to copyright your pages, and include a privacy policy. You can read more about these issues in the chapter, "Plan for Success."

We have talked a lot in this book about providing good content, and of course we are going to talk even more about how to sell your products. But think of your Internet business as a three-legged stool. Content and sales are two of the legs. The third is your mailing list. One of the most important things your web site *must do* is collect names for your list. As you've already learned, 95 percent of your visitors will take a look around and then move on to another web site. They may love your site; they may even bookmark it. How many sites do you have bookmarked on your computer desktop? How many of those have you ever gone back and revisited? Yeah—same for us.

But if you collect your visitor's name and e-mail address, you can write to him and remind him how wonderful your business is. You can offer him reasons to visit again and again, and deals too good to ignore. We discussed some of the practical details of collecting names earlier in this chapter. We talk much more about building and using your mailing list in the chapter, "Get the Word Out."

PHYSICAL CONSTRUCTION OF YOUR SITE

If you happen to be a programmer, you don't need us to tell you how to build your site, at least not in terms of technical skills, but please do read this section carefully for the marketing information.

If you are an average, nontechnical person, the actual physical construction of your site can be done in one of several ways. First, if you are using the web host we recommend, at www.CashMachine Domains.com, you have access to an excellent site building tool. This is known as a WYSIWYG (pronounced "wizzy-wig") tool, which stands for "what you see is what you get." In other words, you do not need to know hypertext markup language (HTML), which is the programming language used on web sites, to dictate instructions on arrangement of text and function. Although it looks much like standard English and is not very difficult to learn, it is no longer necessary for you to be conversant in HTML to build a good basic site.

Another very popular web site building software is Microsoft's FrontPage. FrontPage is part of the basic software package installed on most Windows-based personal computers. If you are familiar with Microsoft Word, you will find FrontPage fairly easy to use. A more complicated but still popular web site building software is Dreamweaver.

We focus on blogs in the next chapter, but this is a good time to introduce you to WordPress. WordPress is an open source (free) software most often used for blogs. Its technology is very attractive to the search engines, and there is a growing trend to design entire sites using WordPress. For example, Jillian and her family operate a number of affiliate sites built in WordPress. Finally, another alternative in constructing your site is to buy a ready-made template (built in FrontPage or WordPress) and then personalize it.

Neither of us is particularly technical in orientation, although of course we have acquired some technical skills along the way. Nevertheless, Jillian builds most of her sites herself in FrontPage. Joe contracts with a webmaster who builds and maintains his sites. As you can imagine, both approaches have their advantages. The best thing about building and maintaining your own site is the ability to make changes instantaneously, without having to wait upon the convenience of another person.

A good middle ground is to hire a contractor to build you a web site template with a variety of different page layouts, perhaps five or six. Then you can simply replace or update text as needed, or change out photographs or graphics to create new pages. You may want your template to include a custom-made header, which can be produced with Adobe PhotoShop, based on ideas you provide.

Rent A Coder (www.RentaCoder.com) is a wonderful resource for the small business owner. You can visit this site and set up an account in a matter of minutes, and look at sample work from contractors in all areas. At Rent A Coder you can hire writers, graphic artists, web site builders, software coders, and experts with a multitude of other skills. These contractors live all over the world. As you probably know, there are very highly skilled technical personnel in India, Pakistan, Romania, Argentina, and a number of other countries where the economies are depressed and jobs are in short supply. Many of these people have organized small companies and cottage industries to bid on jobs through Rent A Coder and similar sites. They do great work at very low cost, and pool their profits to provide good incomes for themselves, relative to their local economies. They often speak excellent English, and it is very easy to communicate with them. Of course, we have also used Rent A Coders from less exotic lands such as Virginia and New Mexico.

To solicit bids from Rent A Coder, simply write a clear explanation of the work you want done, and post it on the site. You can invite specific contractors to bid, or you can offer it for general bidding. You will usually begin receiving bids almost immediately. At Rent A Coder, you can probably have your template pages designed and built for under $50 U.S.

Other Internet businesses provide similar services, such as eLance (www.eLance.com) and Guru (www.Guru.com), but in our experience, Rent A Coder has the lowest overall rates. The best thing about using these services is the ability to see samples of the contractor's work, and to check their ratings from previous jobs. At the end of your job, both you and the contractor will also submit ratings on each other, so of course it is important for you to be professional, courteous, and fair in your dealings with the contractors you use.

THE SINGLE-PAGE SALES SITE

Many people who have one product to sell begin with a single-page sales site. That's an excellent place to start. A single-page site is quick and easy to build, and you can be in business very quickly. Even if you are building a full web site comprised of a number of pages, we recommend you showcase each product with its own individual sales page, and promote the product from that page.

The single-page sales site operates by different rules than a general business web site. In this type of site, your entire emphasis is on the product and the process of inviting your visitor to buy the product. Throw away any superfluous elements. For example, although some sales sites include a graphic header, many do not. Marketers often test response on pages with and without headers to see which design will sell better. In many cases, a simple headline is much more effective.

As we said before, never offer obvious links away from your site (you can have very small links at the bottom to your terms and conditions, privacy policy, and your affiliate program, if applicable). Everything on your site should lead your prospect inexorably down the page to the "Buy Now" link.

Many single-page sales sites are now introduced through a *squeeze page*. The squeeze page is a concept whose history is short and somewhat obscure, but we believe the idea originated with a brilliant Internet marketer named Jonathan Mizel and has subsequently been adopted and popularized by many others. Here's how it works.

The reader follows a link to get information about a product. First, however, he lands on a squeeze page that offers a brief, enticing introduction to the product, then directs the reader to fill out a contact form before moving on to the actual sales page. The benefit of a squeeze page is easy to see: You, the marketer, collect the visitor's e-mail address for your mailing list and can continue to market to him. The potential drawback is also easy to see. Your customer may prefer to leave the page and shop elsewhere, rather than subscribing to yet another mailing list.

You can increase the likelihood your visitor will stay to play by using video or audio on the squeeze page. For example, you might display your photo, and set an audio recording to start five seconds after the page opens, with your voice saying something like "Congratulations! You are about to learn all about XYZ, the very best way to give yourself the gift of beautiful skin. Now please take just a moment and enter your e-mail address below, and we'll take you immediately to more information." Include a little bit of persuasive text, and make the whole process quick and easy.

Research shows that, although some visitors are lost at the squeeze page, there is a higher conversion rate (of visitors to buyers) for those who complete the process. We like squeeze pages and frequently use them. You can see an example at www.Cashfor Writers.com.

Our next guest expert is Internet marketing guru Mark Hendricks. Here he shares with you some of his dynamite formulas for writing the single-page sales site.

GUEST EXPERT ARTICLE

THREE SECRETS TO MAKING YOUR SALES LETTERS SELL

Mark Hendricks

The classic sales letter formula is AIDA, for all you opera lovers: attention, interest, desire, and action. Here are three secrets I've developed for writing sales letters that really sell.

Secret 1: WHOA

This is my "whoa" formula. I got used to saying that around our farm—"Whoa!"

The W stands for people who *want* what you've got. That's the big secret, folks. If you get your message out in front of people who already want what you've got, you're almost there. The problem is you spend most of your time trying to pitch to people who don't want what you've got. Don't even try.

The second element is the *headline* that's going to get their attention. The third thing is the *offer* and the last thing is the call to *action*—WHOA. You can do this on a postcard. You can do it on a web page. You can do it in a sales letter. You can do it in video or audio.

Here's the format: I put in front of somebody who cares a headline to get their attention. I create an offer. "Here's what I'm offering to let you buy, and all of the reasons why." Then I tell them to buy it now.

That's the simple version. Now, let's expand this, starting with headlines. Here's an easy ways to make headlines: Fill in the blanks. Take any headline that gets your attention and take out the operative words, leaving a skeleton that can be filled out in numerous ways.

Let's look at the a familiar one. "How to _Be Prepared_ and _Review_." What's a classic book that used this? *How to Win Friends and Influence People* by Dale Carnegie. That's the headline—how to _____ and _____. In other words, the two benefits: Win friends, influence people.

(Continued)

Secret 2: The Five P's

In your offer, you want to include these five P's:

1. The *promise.* This is a description of your three biggest benefits.
2. Your *product.* Give a detailed description.
3. The *package.* This comprises everything that is part of your offer, including some bonuses. The bonuses should relate to the original product or at least complement it in some way.
4. The *price.* If it's special pricing, make sure you let them know it.
5. The *penalty.* Here's what happens if you don't act right now, whether there is a time limit, a quantity limit, or some other kind of scarcity factor built into it.

Secret 3: Seventeen Psychological Steps

Here is my 17-step formula for successful sales letters, web sites, and ads. I don't always follow this formula, but I always use it as a template to keep myself on track.

Then I'll just make the thing flow. I kind of do it subconsciously nowadays. If you get this, you're going to be able to write a sales letter that makes sense, every time.

Somebody called me up the other day and said, "You know, I've seen you do that 17-step thing and I was going through one of your sales letters. By the time I got done reading, you had answered all of my questions in the sales letter."

I said, "Well, that's what it's supposed to do." In a sales presentation, you want to be revealing information to the prospect when it needs to be revealed. Not before, and not too late. You want to bring up the next question and then answer it, all the way through the process.

Steps 1, 2, and 3 are *preheadline, headline,* and *subheadline.* Headlines are designed to get people's attention. A preheadline is something that happens prior to the main headline. The subheadline is the little stuff that happens underneath that.

Step 4 is to *state the problem.* You got your visitor's attention with the headline, and now you want to capture the imagination. You want to state their problem or the goal that they want to achieve. You also want to establish yourself as the authority in your field. Let them know what makes you an expert, so they know they can trust you.

Step 5 is to *give the solution*. Offer some solution options. You may even want to bring up alternatives to your product. How bold is that, if you actually bring up your competition? Present yours as the best solution. You're going to let them know that you do know the marketplace. You're not trying to hide. "Here are my competitors. They're all good—but here's the best solution."

In step 6 you *give them a sample or tell them a story*. By giving them a free sample, you've immediately got the principle of reciprocation at work—they feel they owe you something, at least their willingness to listen. And why would you want to tell people a story? A story evokes emotion and keeps their attention. It's how humans relate to one another. It also opens the mind so that people will believe you.

If you tell stories, there is a useful concept in theater called *willing suspension of disbelief*. That's kind of an odd way of saying that for the time being, I'm going to pretend what you're telling me is true. So when you're telling a story (I don't mean a lie) or spinning a yarn or whatever you want to call it, that lets people relax so their defenses come down and they will at least be receptive to hear your story.

Step 7 is to name the *benefits*. Tell your readers how they benefit from your product, using a list of benefit bullets. These are like mini-headlines. They go bang, bang, bang, bang.

In your headlines, you probably want to give your three best benefits to get people's attention and lead them into your letter. In your benefit bullets, where you go boom, boom, boom, down the list, you want to give all the secondary benefits. So if people don't get it the first time, in this whole laundry list of benefits, there is going to be something to get them excited enough to keep them going with you.

Have you ever been presented something and you're kind of interested, and all of a sudden you get to a point on a benefit bullet list and you go, "Oh, it does *that*, too?" You catch yourself thinking, "Oh, yeah, I need that, too." Those kinds of things are what help get people over the top and into the buying mode.

(Continued)

Step 8 is to offer *social proof*. Use testimonials to let people know that other people have bought your product and benefited from it.

Step 9 is the *offer*. Make them an offer they can't refuse. Construct an irresistible offer. In other words, make it so good that people would be crazy not to take you up on it if they are a true prospect for what you've got. (If they're not a prospect for what you've got, it doesn't matter what you offer them—they're not going to buy.)

In step 10 you *answer the unasked question*. Give them the reason why you can make them such an irresistible offer. Have you ever been in that position as a buyer where, "Boy, this really sounds good; what a really good deal." Then your final brakes come up, don't they? The red flags are going, "Wait a second. This sounds like it's too good."

Then you need to answer the question: "Here's how we can do it." You kind of let them in on your business so they know why you can make such a good deal.

Step 11 is all about *bonuses*. Sweeten the deal. Pile on just a little bit and add some more bonuses. Don't go outrageous with it, though. Have you ever seen situations where people pile on so many bonuses that the deal is worth ten times what the product was worth to begin with? It becomes unbelievable at that time, doesn't it? But do sweeten the deal. It should relate to or somehow complement the original product.

Step 12 is to offer the *guarantee*. Take away the risks. Give them the strongest guarantee possible—the longer the guarantee, the better. If you give somebody a three-day guarantee, guess what they're going to be doing for the next three days? Trying to break your product or show that it doesn't work. They're going to spend all their time focusing on that. If you give them seven days, they will spend time trying to figure it out.

If you give them 30 days, chances are they don't remember what they did 14 days ago. I'm not saying that you're trying to trick anybody out of money. I'm just telling you that human nature is such that if you give people a short fuse to work with, they will spend all their waking hours and some of their sleeping hours trying to see if they want to keep your product.

So, the longer your guarantee—60 days, 90 days, one year—the better. Can you remember what you bought a year ago? It just falls into the "a lot of stuff" category, right?

Step 13 is about creating *scarcity*. If it's limited in supply, tell them. They'll want it even more.

Step 14 is to *ask for the order,* and step 15 is to *state the consequences* of not ordering. Tell them exactly how to order. Tell them exactly what happens if they don't order now. Where I learned this was from going to the doctor. You don't think of doctors as being sales-people, do you? Believe me, they are.

Now I'm sure doctors are typically looking out for your best interests. If you go in and there's something seemingly wrong (I'm not talking about the sniffles), they want to do tests. The tests come back, and you come back into the office. It wasn't one of those things where they call up and say, "Everything is okay. Don't worry about it." It's "When you come back in . . ."

So now you're back in the office. Their first words, they look at the chart and go, "Hmmm." Okay, now you've got my attention. All you had to do was say that headline: "Hmmm . . ."

Then Doc explains what the problem is. "Here's what the tests say." The catcher is when they say, "Now, if we don't do anything, here's what's going to happen." It's a great example of using this principle. It's "Here's what I recommend that we do. Now you know what's wrong. You know that the good news is we can fix it." Sign up here. Buy now and everything is going to be okay.

Then you hesitate and they say, "Oh, by the way, I forgot to tell you. Here's what happens if we don't take care of this." That's when they really get your attention, right? Then it's a matter of "How soon can I get in to get whatever it is done?"

Step 16 is to add your *signature.* Sign off with a friendly and heartfelt close, and use your signature. How do you use your signature on a web page? Use a felt-tip pen or something that's some-what bold to write your signature. Now, you may only want to use your first name or something because some people are sneaky. They may somehow get your signature and do funny things with it. Don't use your banking signature, obviously. I just use my first name.

(Continued)

Then you scan that and you save it as a jpeg image. Then you place it on your web page below where you say "Sincerely," and there's your signature, right underneath.

Step 17 is to add *postscripts*. Use a P.S. to summarize all the points. You may use one postscript or two or more. The order to follow is P.S., P.P.S. P.P.P.S, and so on. The first postscript can be used to restate your offer. The second is to remind them of what happens if they don't buy. The third is to tell them to take action now.

Those are the 17 steps. If you would like to look at one of my sales letters, and identify for yourself each of these steps, there is a good example at www.YouAskThem.com.

© **2007 Mark Hendricks. Used by permission.**

Mark Hendricks is an Internet entrepreneur, business coach, author, and software developer. His web sites include www.hunteridge.com, www.internet-success-system .com, www.market-soft.com, www.SwiftKickintheButt.com and www .ScientificAdvertisinginthe21stCentury.com

Resource Page

Summary of topics discussed in this chapter:
☛ Equipment you need for your Internet business.
☛ How to select your URL.
☛ Finding the best web host.
☛ Setting up your infrastructure.
☛ Designing your web site.
☛ Physical construction of your site.
☛ How to set up the single-page sales site.

This chapter also includes an article by guest expert Mark Hendricks on secrets to make your sales letters sell.

Go to www.YourInternetCashMachine.com and find much more information on setting up your web site, as well as interviews with our guest experts. Claim your free membership now!

GET THE WORD OUT

However attractive your web site, however persuasive your sales copy, however fascinating the content, nothing happens until potential customers find you. Marketing is the process of disseminating information about your business so that visitors will come to your site.

In Internet-speak, those visitors are *traffic*. Traffic, properly managed, becomes your *list*. Readers on that list become your customers.

This chapter shows you the action steps of marketing your business.

E-MAIL MARKETING

The basis of most Internet businesses is e-mail marketing. Internet marketers are fond of saying, "The money is in the list," but our friend Craig Perrine (www.MaverickMarketer.com) takes issue with that. Craig likes to say, "The money is in your relationship with your list." We concur. Building a friendly, trustworthy relationship with the people on your list is critical to the success of your business.

The e-mails you send to your list should first of all reflect your personality. Write as you would to a friend, in your own distinctive voice. You may never think of your *voice*, in the way that writers use the term. But if you ask people who know you well, they will readily identify the expressions you use and the patterns of your speech.

Secondly, your e-mail must communicate a sense of your competence and authority. You are the expert in your field, and you have knowledge your readers hope to gain. Write to your readers as equals, with respect, but don't be shy about positioning yourself as a leader.

Ideally, each e-mail you send to your list will combine that sense of your personality and authority with some useful information, and possibly a touch of humor. Occasionally your e-mail will include some personal news or refer your reader to your latest article or blog entry. But here are the two things that should be included in 99.5 percent of your e-mails:

1. An offer.
2. A call to action.

Your business is selling. Your readers understand that, and you should, too. In the past, we were sometimes reticent to sell in every e-mail, and reluctant to send e-mails more than a couple of times a week. In the past few years, we have learned better. Now we e-mail our lists daily throughout the work week, and we are selling more than ever. Rather than resenting the frequency of e-mails, our readers seem grateful for the opportunity to know us better and to receive useful offers from us. The occasional reader who is ready to move on unsubscribes from our lists, but the overwhelming number of readers remain on our lists, open our e-mails, and buy from us.

To learn how to write compelling e-mails, see Make it Hypnotic!.

ARTICLES

Articles are a terrific way to get traffic to your web site. Think about a variety of topics that will be of interest to your readers, and write a series of 500- to 700-word articles. Be creative with your headlines, as many people will only read the headline and skim the actual article. Your headline should include the keyword or keywords you want to use. At the bottom of the article include a contact box with your name, your web site, and the offer of an ethical bribe.

Post your articles on article distribution sites. You can find these by typing in "article directories" in your search engine. A good source is www.UltimateArticleDirectory.com. Here are some of the top web sites that publish articles for republication by other sites:

- www.A1Articles.com
- www.ArticleBin.com
- www.ArticleCity.com
- www.ArticleDepot.co.uk
- www.Amazines.com
- www.EzineArticles.com
- www.GoArticles.com
- www.IdeaMarketers.com
- www.Isnare.com
- www.SearchWarp.com

Software is available that will make the publication of your articles quicker and simpler. We've provided more information for you on our web site, www.YourInternetCashMachine.com. Check the Resource page at the end of this chapter for details.

In the chapter, "Set Up Your Web Site," we introduced you to RentaCoder.com and other freelance web sites. There are a number of excellent writers available who can write articles for you for a very affordable fee. You simply provide them with the subject and the content. If needed, they can also research for additional content. You can search on Rent A Coder to get an idea what fees have been charged by various writers for similar projects, and what ratings the writers have been awarded by previous clients.

You will be amazed at the power of articles. Once you submit a few, and they are accepted by the article directories, newsletters and other sites throughout the world will begin to republish them, along with your contact box. The links back to your site will improve your standing in the search engines, and many new visitors will sign up for your mailing list. Finally, include your articles as content on your web site.

SEARCH ENGINE OPTIMIZATION

It is useful for your business to be highly ranked in the search engines, particularly if your listing appears on the first three pages. Before the advent of Google, search engines such as Yahoo! simply categorized sites according to descriptions submitted by the site owner. Site designers packed their pages with meta tags, hidden keywords visible only to the search engines. Visitors who used the search engine entered their search criteria and accessed a database of home pages based on these keywords and descriptions.

The founders of Google took that model and stood it on its head. Google's formulas are proprietary, and the company guards them like the U.S. Treasury guards Fort Knox. However, students of the process have studied Google and made some observations that are useful. As of this writing, Google is the most popular search engine, but it is of course not the only one. It is safe to say, however, that all the search engines are now using ranking techniques similar to those of Google.

Google does not simply categorize sites by their home pages. Instead, Google allows its users to search a subject based on every page of every site in its directory, so that it accesses literally billions of pages. According to the best guess of the Google-watchers, Google employs a two-part formula to rank web sites. Part 1 is *page rank*, which denotes the relative importance of a site and each of its pages to the World Wide Web. Part 2 is *relevance rank*, which assesses the relevance of any web page to a particular search.

The search engines use software called *crawlers* or *spiders* to review your web site and collect information toward your page rank and relevance rank. Google's spider is called the *Googlebot*. The best way to ensure the spiders keep visiting your site and update your information is by adding valuable content. To help the spiders, always link to new content from your home page.

If you want to be highly ranked by the search engines, and of course you do, you must have a blog. We go into this subject in greater detail in the next section of this chapter.

At http://Toolbar.Google.com, you can download the Google Toolbar, a free accessory that displays the page rank of web sites on a logarithmic scale of 1 to 10. If you site's rank is zero, it is not included in Google's database. The most highly ranked sites are ranked between 8 and 10, while a page rank of 5 to 7 connotes strong content. If your site is ranked between 1 and 4, you still have work to do.

You have undoubtedly seen ads, and perhaps received e-mails, from search engine optimization (SEO) businesses that promise to raise your rankings in the search engines. In our opinion, there is little value in working with such firms. Instead, we encourage you to concentrate on and implement the following recommendations, which represent the best current thinking as to how to achieve a high ranking in the search engines.

Content and Design

Okay, we know we are becoming a bit repetitive here. But we promise, we are doing so for your own good. We want to see your web site appear on those coveted first three pages. So, once again, fill your web site with high-quality information, and emphasize content over design. Avoid using Flash, Java applets, and other fancy bells and whistles. Make navigation easy, both for your customers and for the search engine spiders. Keep your links at the top and the right of the page.

Page Title

Give every page on your site a title, and make the titles relevant to your target keywords. Be sure the title on the page matches the title displayed in the browser. You can use your business name as part of your title, for branding and consistency, but expand it with additional information, page by page. For example, if your business name is Harley Plastics, you may have a page titled "Harley Plastics—Our Product Guarantee," and another titled "Harley Plastics—Our Patented Extrusion Process."

As you write your headers and text copy, use your keywords whenever appropriate. A logical repetition of keywords increases the likelihood the search engines will assess your site as relevant to your desired topic. Avoid overuse of keywords, however. The search engines will penalize you for *keyword packing*. Just be sure your copy makes sense and reads easily.

Also, make sure your links are based on real and relevant words, not some obscure numbering system. When the search engine spiders visit, a meaningless page name will not raise the relevance scores of your web site.

Incoming Links

Incoming links from sites relevant to yours are an extremely powerful tool for raising your search engine ranking. We have recommended you write articles that include a link to your site; write just a few articles and these links will soon appear all over the World Wide Web.

Also, whenever possible, encourage other sites to link to you with descriptive links, rather than simply using your web site URL. For example, a link that says "Learn How to Find and Write Grants!" will be interpreted by the search engines as more relevant than a link that says simply "www.GrantMeRich.com." You can assist other site owners in using the links most beneficial to you by providing them with HTML code for your preferred phrase. For example, you can have a "Link to Us" page where you include the code for cutting and pasting.

You have probably seen links from one site to another displayed in graphical format (for example, as a photograph or drawing). Graphical links are not as beneficial in terms of the search engines as are text links.

The search engines will accord greater weight to incoming links from sites that have a theme similar to or complementary to yours, or sites that are well known and themselves highly ranked. This is a case in which you are known by the company you keep, so exercise some discrimination in terms of accepting incoming links. Your page rank will be adversely affected if you have links to your site from so-called *link farms*, sites that have dozens or even hundreds of outgoing links.

Because your page rank is based on a shared computation, and because you are not penalized for the number of outgoing links you have, you may want to offer useful links to your visitors. Remember, however, that every link away from your site is an invitation to your visitor to head out that back door and quite possibly never return. Once again we suggest, if you include links, put them together on a page of their own.

YOUR BLOG

Have we mentioned that content is king on the Internet? We're sure by now you have filled your web site with valuable content and written many articles. But there is no substitute for having your own blog, for a number of reasons.

Blogs are tremendously attractive to the search engines. They create ongoing content that is added on a regular basis, so the spiders keep coming back and updating your listings. Also, because your readers can subscribe to your blog through RSS (which, you will remember from the chapter, "Select the Best Business Model for You," is *pull* technology), you will be able to stay in touch with many readers outside the vicissitudes of the e-mail system.

There are several platforms for blogs. Among them are Blogger (www .Blogger.com),which is owned by Google, and Typepad (www.Typepad .com). Both Blogger and Typepad are hosted on the Internet. Movable Type (www.MovableType.org), Blogsite (www.Blogsite.com), and Word-Press (www.WordPress.org) are software you install on your own server.

We recommend WordPress, which is an open source software. That simply means it was developed and offered free over the Internet, and a community of developers continues to create and share new utility programs, called plug-ins, that increase its functionality and flexibility. As we described in the chapter, "Set Up Your Web Site," WordPress templates can be used not just for blogs but even for entire sites. If your web server company offers Fantastico, they can help you install and use WordPress. Our preferred web host, accessible through www .CashMachineDomains.com, can easily accommodate and assist you with WordPress. If you need additional help, you can find a technician familiar with WordPress through Rent A Coder.

Many site owners are reluctant to start blogs because they are not really writers, and they don't want to have to produce content every week or two. It is certainly true that many blogs contain wonderful writing and read like the best newspaper or magazine columns.

Many other blogs, however, are just notes written to the readers, much like a brief e-mail. Some site owners simply send out e-mails to notify readers of a new blog posting, and put the meat of all their communications with their list into the blog itself. The authors of this book use our blogs to share personal and business news with readers. You can get ideas by visiting our blogs, at www.MrFire.com and www .GrantMeRich.com. While you're visiting, sign up to receive our blog postings via RSS.

If you are a one-man band, you may be the designated blogger. However, you might be able to interest a spouse or even a contract employee in doing the writing. If you have employees, you might delegate this task. Some companies even designate different employees to write about different aspects of the business, and make the blog a rotating task.

BRANDING

A key concept of marketing is *branding*. Now that you have selected a name for your business, your job is to put that name into the public consciousness and keep it there. Use the name constantly. Create a signature file with the name, and use it every time you send an e-mail. Include the name in the signature file you use when you visit forums or make comments on blogs. Hire a graphic designer (another job for Rent A Coder, perhaps) and create a logo to complement the name. Choose a great font, and combine the logo and printed name into a jpeg file you can display around your web site and on your product covers. A memorable logo goes a long way toward branding a business.

Put your logo and name on your business cards and stationery. Put it on postcards you send out to customers. Use it at the top of online newsletters. If you speak in public, or give radio or television interviews, be sure and mention the name of your business, and link it with your own. Sometimes, if you are your company's primary representative or if your personal services are the company's primary product, the name you brand may be your own. Don't be shy. Graceful self-promotion is at the heart of marketing. After all, as your wise grandmother may have also said, "If you don't blow your own horn, who will?"

JOINT VENTURES

A joint venture (JV), for our purposes, is an agreement between two Internet marketers, one of whom agrees to endorse and promote the other's products or services. Here we will call them the endorser and the endorsee.

Many Internet marketers got started building their lists by entering into joint ventures with other site owners. For example, when Jillian offered her first few classes, Joe was her endorser. He sent out e-mails to his list recommending the classes. In return, Jillian paid Joe a percentage of the tuition for every one of his customers who enrolled. She entered into similar JVs with other site owners and, over a few months, built up a list of her own. Joint ventures continue to be a lucrative source of income for each of us.

There are various types of joint ventures. The endorser can use an e-mail or an e-mail series sent out to his list to sell the endorsee's product.

Joint ventures can be done through teleconferences, usually combined with e-mails. The endorser interviews the endorsee by telephone, over a teleconference line, and invites his readers to listen. An endorser can also display the endorsee's banners or links on his site, or offer a coupon to promote the endorsee's offers. In most cases, the endorsee collects the orders and payments, sends out the merchandise if necessary, and then pays the endorser.

Sometimes JV partners will develop a product together or offer companion products. They can bundle products and offer them as a package. There are as many kinds of joint ventures as there are creative ideas generated by the partners. Everything on the Internet is constantly growing and changing, and we are limited only by our imaginations.

The benefits of a joint venture to the endorser are income, of course, and the opportunity to offer new products. In addition, your readers are always interested in having you tell them about new opportunities, as long as these are congruent with your primary business message. Finally, a joint venture brings a new relationship with the potential for reciprocity.

Chief among the benefits to the endorsee is access to new, prequalified customers. If you are selling a product related to real estate, and you enter into a JV with someone who has a list of real estate investors, chances are high some of those readers will be interested in your product. They may choose to buy or not to buy, and they will form their own opinions about you and your product after they hear you and visit your site. But they are prequalified—they are not on the Internet to buy shoes.

Joint ventures offer much higher potential conversion rates than cold sales. Statistics show the overall standard conversion rate for Internet sales is 2 percent. As we mentioned earlier, the conversion rate refers to the number of sales of a product, divided by the number of people who came and looked at the product. So if 100 people come and look at your sales page, 2 people might buy, in the general order of things. On a teleconference in a joint venture, conversion rates run about 15 percent.

Another benefit to the endorsee is traffic, and it is understood by the endorser that he is sharing his traffic. There are a number of ways you can gain access to the traffic of your JV partners. On the conservative side, you may offer a sign-up box to the visitors to your sales page. In a more aggressive mode, you may set up a squeeze page to collect e-mail addresses before visitors can access the sales page. The endorsee may also set up a registration page for a teleconference, if one is planned, and use a the registration page as a squeeze page to collect e-mail addresses. Once the visitor registers, he is taken to the information he needs to access the teleconference.

Your JV relationships can be of immense value to you, so you want to respect the preferences of your endorsers. Different site owners will vary as to how protective they are with their lists. But even in a case where the endorser does not want you to use a squeeze page of any kind, you will always pick up some new people for your list. The endorser's readers will see what you have to offer, and some of them will decide to go to your site and get more information.

There are some standard conventions that cover the compensation structure for joint ventures. Generally speaking, 40 to 50 percent of any sale generated through a joint venture will be paid to the endorser. When the product is a class, or some other item that involves exceptional time or investment on the part of the endorsee, the endorser may be paid 30 percent of the proceeds of the sale.

Frequently when we are doing a joint venture, we will just send our JV partner a check, or make a payment into his or her PayPal account. However, some JV partners prefer to be set up as regular affiliates through the endorsee's affiliate program. They are then able to go online and check their statistics to see how many sales they have made and how much money they are due. Successful joint ventures often turn into long-term affiliate relationships, in which both parties consistently promote each other's products.

There are many ways to find a JV partner. Using the search engines, look for site owners whose readers will be interested in your products. If you are selling automobile seat covers, for example, look for web sites related to cars and car accessories. When you find a likely site, determine whether the site owner has a mailing list. Amazingly, many web site owners do not. If they are simply an affiliate sales site, they may well not collect names. However, if you see a sign-up box or the offer of a newsletter, chances are the owner has a list of people who may be interested in your products or services. A list of any number over 1,000 people is a potential market for you. Then approach the site owner with an idea as to how you can make money together.

Some people who do business on the Internet haven't quite grasped the cooperative business model. So you may encounter some who will say, "Well, my site is in competition with yours, so I don't want to do a joint venture." Sometimes you have to educate people a little bit. It's a learning curve, especially for folks who have left the traditional business world or expanded from traditional business to the Internet.

Newsgroups, forums, and message boards may be another source of joint venture partners. Networking is always one of your most powerful tools for accessing partners. Ask fellow marketers for referrals. The more people you know doing business online, regardless of whether the other businesses are remotely related to yours, the greater your pool of resources.

Existing JV partners are also a good source of referrals for new joint ventures. If your current or previous partners trust you and are comfortable with you, they will probably be happy to introduce you to new partners.

There are now a number of JV brokers, who represent a new and growing business model on the Internet. Brokers will put you in touch with potential JV partners. They may charge 10 percent for an introduction. The charge may be as much as 15 to 20 percent if they are going to provide assistance with the deal, such as setting up the date, giving you the teleconference lines, and writing some e-mails. The use of JV brokers is a perfectly viable way of doing business. Find out what their reputation is. Look at their agreements and be sure that you're comfortable with them.

Often new marketers will meet established web site business owners at conferences, and these contacts may eventually result in joint venture relationships. If you're meeting someone at a seminar, you might have only a few minutes to establish contact. Since it is likely that your list is much smaller than his, and you are an unknown quantity to that person, we recommend you simply introduce yourself and say a little bit about what you do. Then ask for permission to contact them again. You might say, "Could we exchange cards? Do you mind if I call you sometime when you have a few minutes, so we can talk?"

We've found that Internet marketers are incredibly generous with advice, support, and time. Perhaps that's because we are all relatively new to the business. Even those of us who have been on the Internet the longest only have 12 years or so under our belts. We have all learned from other people. That spirit of cooperation is one of the things we most enjoy about working on the Internet.

But people are also clearheaded about the business proposition. So an established marketer is probably not, in two minutes, going to commit himself to sending to his list of 50,000 people news about your new product that may or may not do very well. But if he knows you and thinks you're a nice person, he will be open to finding out more. This may be particularly true if you say, "I'd love to ask you a couple of questions. I'd love to learn a little more from you."

Established marketers are frequently approached for joint ventures, and we do want joint ventures. We are not resting on our laurels. We want to make more money tomorrow, and JVs are a way to do it. But intelligent marketers are always discriminating about joint ventures. We are protective of our lists, and we only want to offer our readers products and services in which they will be genuinely interested.

When you consider approaching a well-established, successful site owner, think of it as you do dating. (If you haven't dated in a while, dredge around in your memory.) When you see an attractive person across a crowded room, you don't just walk over and say, "Will you have my children?" You may walk over and say, "Would you like to have a cup of coffee after the meeting?"

If you find somebody with whom you want to do a JV, sign up for her list. Learn her *unique selling proposition* (USP). Find out about her philosophy of business. What is she doing? What are her values? What is her communication style? Really get to know the person before you approach her. Determine how you can add value for her list. Think to yourself, if I were she, what would I be looking for from a partner? How can I make this a good deal for the other person?

Figure out how to make the deal easy for your potential endorser. If you can make it easy, and make her money, chances are she will see the advantage of working with you. For example, if you want to have a teleconference, offer to make all the arrangements.

Different people like to be contacted in different ways, but generally, the following is a pretty safe approach. E-mail the person first and suggest a time for a phone meeting. In your e-mail, introduce yourself and explain what benefits you would bring to a joint venture. Show him you are a person he might want to pay attention to and with whom he may want to do business.

Then suggest a time for a phone meeting. If you don't get an early positive response, write a letter on your letterhead and send it via FedEx to show him you are a professional person. Send a clear proposal. In plain English, write a very clear idea of what you envision doing. Show that you are familiar with and admire his work. He is going to be completely uninterested in working with you if you just cold-call him without any clear indication of what you are doing. You are wasting his time. Show that you have already identified him as a real potential partner. Then, introduce yourself, your service, and your products.

Give statistics, especially conversion rates from previous offers. Show your potential partner that it's likely that he will make money doing business with you. Emphasize the benefits to him. Highlight the ease and convenience you can offer. Provide a free copy of your product. He'll do the same for you. That enables you to be very sure that you are not offering a substandard product to your list, and the other person has the same protection.

Offer the affiliate program, if desired. Some people want to be signed up to an affiliate program, while others want to just make the call or send an e-mail and be sent a check. Offer a brief letter of agreement if the person asks for it. Frankly, we've had very few letters of agreement on joint ventures, but sometimes people prefer them.

In a joint venture, quality counts on both sides. The endorsee must offer quality and the endorser must review the product and ensure quality. If you as endorser do a JV with somebody whose product is inferior, and nine people on your list buy that product and are unhappy, two things may happen. Number one, many of those nine people will return the product and request refunds. And, number two, do you think you will ever sell anything again to those nine people? You have burned those customers.

Put the customer first, always. Act with absolute integrity. Your reputation and the reputation of your JV partner are on the line. It is a matter of self-interest. You are building relationships you can have for a long time, and if things go well, you can continue making money together.

YOUR AFFILIATE PROGRAM

Just as affiliate sales sites are a powerful vehicle for selling products on the Internet, so will your business be greatly multiplied if you have a well-managed affiliate program for your products. As we discussed earlier, affiliate software is included in www.CashMachineCart.com. This software is quite easy to use and comes with tutorials. You can set the parameters as to whether you must preapprove affiliates, designate which products they may sell, and determine the commission they will receive.

Many Internet business owners eventually contract with affiliate managers who run their affiliate programs for a percentage of sales.

NEWSLETTERS

In addition to e-mail communications with your list and blog postings, you may want to publish an online newsletter (or even an off-line one, as you'll read later in the chapter). Some marketers send their newsletters via e-mail, but we recommend you create an HTML web page just for the newsletter. Joe's monthly newsletter, *News You Can Use*, is very popular with his readers. He posts it on the Internet, then e-mails his list to let them know it is available.

NEWSGROUPS

A good way to let people know about your site is to hang out in newsgroups, or forums, related to your topic. Forum etiquette prohibits overt advertising and self-promotion, but it is perfectly appropriate to offer pertinent comments and suggestions, and to include your signature and web site address. Over time, you will gain credibility and people will begin to visit your site for more ideas.

PRESS RELEASES/PUBLIC RELATIONS

Press releases are an excellent way to let the public know about all the developments in your business, including the release of new products. PRWeb (www.PRWeb.com) is an online press release service that offers several levels of service, both free and paid. PRWeb can distribute your press release to thousands of media outlets both online and off-line. Similar sites include www.Press-Release-Writing.com, and www.PRFree.com. Tips on writing an effective press release are available at our web site, www.YourInternetCashMachine.com.

One of the unique aspects of having an Internet business is the relative ease with which you can become known as an expert in your field. Because readers all over the world will visit your site and value your ideas, your opinions will be respected. By all means, take every opportunity to foster your reputation as an expert. Producing information products in your field, perhaps even writing a book, will help you build your reputation. Radio, television, and print interviews are a great way to publicize yourself and your business.

GUEST EXPERT ARTICLE

PUBLICITY SECRETS TO ATTAIN MASSIVE SUCCESS FOR YOUR INTERNET BUSINESS

Annie Jennings

Want to know the ultimate secret to massive success as an Internet marketer? Here it is: Be everywhere at all times. If you're not making more money than you can spend, then you're not doing it right!

Publicity allows you to be everywhere at all times. Publicity offers nonstop ways to be seen and be heard by your target audience over and over again. You can get booked for interviews on radio shows in big cities or on national radio shows, appear in major newspapers and magazines with huge circulation, get booked as the guest on high-powered national TV shows reaching millions with your message, and lots more. The key is to reach out to your audience consistently using these powerful publicity outlets. The *secret* key is to be everywhere at all times!

Radio Interviews

Radio interviews offer excellent outreach to thousands of listeners. For best results, interviews should be in the major top 50 cites in the country and on the nationally syndicated shows. The top 50

(Continued)

markets include New York City; Los Angeles; Chicago; Philadelphia; Boston; Washington, D.C.; Atlanta; and lots more. These major markets are the highest in population, offering you a much greater outreach than an interview in a smaller market. The regional and nationally syndicated shows are distributed to dozens, hundreds, and even thousands of stations and reach a myriad of cities across the country, giving you huge exposure nationally while reaching your smaller cities and communities at the same time.

Yes, you can mention your web site on radio shows! This is one venue where you can mention your web site and promote your book or products as long as you give a great interview. Offer a content-rich interview that provides great benefit to the listener. If they like you and your message, they will be more likely to want to visit your site to find out more and stay connected with you. Another advantage of getting booked as the guest on a radio show is that you can do the interview from anywhere in the country, or even the world, as it is usually conducted via telephone.

Television

Appearing on local, regional, and national TV helps you create a powerful platform along with celebrity appeal and national expert status for yourself. A powerful platform is critical for your Internet business to be deemed a credible and trusted source of products and services.

Print

Print media includes newspapers, magazines, wire services, newsletters, and journals. Many print media placements include a quote or two from you as the expert, as well as the name of your book, product, or company. Many newsletters and trade journals accept articles written by you in which you can showcase your knowledge and talent, plus they allow an "about the author" section at the end of the article that can include your contact info, phone number, and web site. Also, major newspapers and magazines have online versions of their publications that can link back to your site, which of course can drive numerous new visitors to your site.

Internet

Internet placements are great not only for providing massive outreach but also because, when potential clients do an Internet search on your company, your big online placements come up in the search results, increasing your credibility and status. Go after placements on impressive sites that everyone knows, but keep in mind that many other web sites accept content-driven articles that can also include your contact info and even link back to your site. Internet placements and online articles are excellent for visibility, outreach, search engine optimization, and especially for driving lots of new visitors to your web site.

Conversion Strategy

As you are driving lots of visitors to your site, it is essential to have a conversion strategy in place that guides your visitors to a desired outcome—which, by the way, may not initially be a sale. Keep in mind that sales come later, after your visitors gain trust in you and discover their need for your products or services.

Podcasting

Podcasting is a great way to reach new markets. Your podcast strategy should lead the listener back to your site by offering lots of value-added goodies. Don't overly promote your products or services on your podcast. Remember, just one or two promotions per podcast are enough.

Teleseminars

Your teleseminars should be content-rich, demonstrating your talent and expertise, and designed to empower your listeners with new skills and knowledge that allow them to excel. The key to sales is to build credibility and trust through sharing your knowledge for the betterment of all—and, of course, having products or services your market actually wants to purchase.

(Continued)

E-Zine/E-Mail Newsletter

Every Internet business should have an e-zine or e-mail newsletter that is packed with valuable info and not overly promotional for products or services. Remember the key to success is to gain the respect of your community by always offering content-rich information that addresses their needs. You can inform your subscribers about your services and products, but do it discreetly. They know what you sell, and when they need it they will come to you.

Know Your Web Site Stats

Web stats (the number of visitors, the paths they took on your site, the pages they visited, their exit pages, the keywords they used to find your site, etc.) are critical as they reveal which strategies are working, allowing you to make the necessary strategy changes to improve your results. Are visitors leaving after viewing just one page? You might need a strategy that offers them a reason to stay on your site. Are they visiting your shopping cart but not buying? This is information you need to know.

Data Capture Strategy

Everyone who comes to your site should be offered the opportunity to join your community by giving you their name and e-mail address so you can keep in touch via your e-mail newsletter.

Want to make more money than you can spend? Remember, the market sends you messages—people are either buying your products and services or they are not. If you are not making more money than you can spend, it's time to revisit your overall marketing and publicity strategy to identify areas to build, to change, to tweak, to empower.

Want massive publicity success? Visit www.anniejenningspr.com for lots of free special reports, publicity strategy CDs, and audio recordings that all reveal insider publicity tips to empower you to get massive publicity!

> *Annie Jennings is the founder of the national public relations firm Annie Jennings PR, and is a national publicist specializing in promoting authors and experts to the media. Annie Jennings has over 25,000 authors and experts signed up with her company. Want to be an Annie Jennings PR expert? Let Annie know all about you and your PR objectives at www.anniejenningspr.com/experts.htm and get your free Optimal PR Strategy CD as a special thank you.*

TELESEMINARS AND WEBINARS

As we discussed concerning joint ventures, teleseminars are a great sales promotional tool. You can also use teleseminars to provide information to your readers and the readers of other lists; you can charge for these seminars or offer them free. Either way, you can record them and use the recordings as information products.

Webinars are a technology that combines both audio and visual presentations. Your audience members call in on a predetermined phone number, then also go to a special web site, where they can view your presentation as they listen to the call.

Promote your teleseminars and webinars with classified ads on eBay, through press releases, or through other lists. Visit www.Your InternetCashMachine.com for teleseminar and webinar resources.

Guest expert Jim Edwards believes in entertaining his viewers, and his *Friday Night Smackdown* videos keep us laughing while we learn. He is at the forefront of marketers using webinar technology.

GUEST EXPERT ARTICLE

WEBINARS—THE FUTURE OF ONLINE MARKETING

Jim Edwards

The next logical step for the Internet involves moving closer to interactive television.

People love to watch TV, they love to surf the Web, and tens of millions enjoy interacting with other people on social networking web sites like MySpace.com.

(Continued)

Now imagine if you could combine all of these elements people enjoy so much into a single technology that enabled you to bring together up to 1,000 people in one place to teach, demonstrate, sell, and interact—all without anyone leaving their home or office.

Well you can, and this technology is called a *webinar!* Though webinar technology has existed for almost a decade, for most of that time it remained strictly the domain of well-funded high-tech companies. However, as with most killer apps online, advances in technology now place powerful webinar capabilities within reach of virtually any businessperson.

Webinars enable you to make presentations to up to 1,000 people or more at once using audio and video elements.

Though webinar technology has advanced greatly, delivering the audio and video components together through the Web still lacks stability. I've personally found using a telephone conference line to deliver the webinar audio much more effective than trying to stream the audio live through the Web.

As for interactivity, webinars allow you to chat live with viewers, conduct real-time surveys (polls), and see exactly which of your customers and prospects attend your live webinar. So not only can you see exactly which of your hot prospects attend your webinar, you can chat directly with them, answer their questions live, and poll the group for valuable feedback in real time.

Over the past few months, many of my subscribers and customers have asked me basically the same question: "What groups of people will benefit the most by using webinar technology?" My answer: Anyone who would normally make any type of public presentation in front of a group of two or more people in a boardroom, meeting room, or convention center can benefit immediately by using webinars.

The following examples will help you see the power of webinars to help make sales, develop information products, and save a fortune on travel expenses.

☞ A salesperson who travels all over the country giving the same presentation over and over could use webinars to make that presentation without leaving her office.

☞ A software developer or marketer could use webinars to demonstrate his new software and receive immediate feedback from existing or potential customers.

☞ A trainer could make a webinar presentation to her customers and prospects, record it, and turn it into a valuable info product for sale or archive it as an on-demand training program.

☞ A speaker could create a series of paid webinars and deliver them live to customers all over the world, earning speaking fees without ever enduring airport security again.

☞ An affiliate marketer could use webinars to demonstrate products for vendors and earn commissions from products they didn't even create.

Any company, large or small, that sells virtually any product or service online can benefit from adding webinars to its online marketing arsenal. In fact, any online businessperson who fails to do so risks putting himself at a serious disadvantage.

© **Jim Edwards. All rights reserved. Used with permission.**

Jim Edwards is a syndicated newspaper columnist and the co-creator of a step-by-step, paint-by-numbers coaching program that guarantees to teach you how to go from zero to making real money online with your own webinars. Access his insider secrets at http://www.WebinarSecrets.com/special/

OTHER WAYS TO INCREASE TRAFFIC AND GROW YOUR LIST

Audio and Video Recordings

You can also upload recordings of teleseminars and make them available as podcasts, or specifically record podcasts to make them downloadable from your web site or through iTunes. In addition, you can now post video infomercials on a variety of sites, such as www.YouTube.com, www.BlipTV.com, www.VideoEgg.com, and www.DailyMotion.com.

Viral Products

Viral products, such as e-books, reports, and software, are created to be shared around the Internet. They provide genuine value, and users enjoy sharing them with others. They are coded with the Internet business web site brand.

Rebrandable Products

Products can also be created that allow purchasers to rebrand them for resale or to use as gifts. This mechanism encourages broad distribution throughout the Internet.

Cross Promotions

During the past couple of years, Internet marketers have been supporting each other in promoting books, new products, and events through cross promotions. During the launch, a buyer who purchases the product can also access a number of bonuses submitted by other marketers. In order to download the free bonus, the customer goes through a squeeze page and subscribes to the list of the marketer offering the bonus.

Your Own Forum

You may want to consider offering a forum on your own web site, particularly if your topic is one of wide interest. Your forum will attract new readers to your site. If your web host offers Fantastico software, you can easily set up a forum.

Testimonials

A good way to become better known on the Internet, and thus attract more traffic to your site, is to offer testimonials. When you use a product you like, or if you read a book you admire, send in an insightful testimonial, along with your photograph and site information. You can also write book reviews for books on Amazon (www.Amazon.com).

Buy/Trade Advertising

You can buy either graphic or text ads on other web sites, and also trade advertising with other site owners. Again, as mentioned earlier, we recommend ads that include text links rather than graphical links.

Exit Traffic

Exit traffic sign-ups are the flip side of squeeze pages. If your visitor has not subscribed to your list prior to leaving, you can set up a "fly in" sign-up box with a compelling offer.

Offers to Unsubscribers

Fellow Internet marketer Mark Hendricks has a wonderful technique for the folks he calls his "loyal unsubscribers." We love the idea and thought we'd share it with you. When one of his readers decides to leave his list, and clicks the "Unsubscribe" link at the bottom of an e-mail, the reader is invited to instead take advantage of a deep discount to purchase a product. If the reader declines, he receives a friendly "thank you and goodbye."

Free Reports Tied to Keywords

Once you determine the keywords that bring you the best traffic, you can offer free reports to surfers who search those keywords.

Pay per Click

One of the quickest, most dependable ways to get more targeted traffic is to buy it, using pay-per-click (PPC) programs such as the one offered by Google.

Our next guest expert, Simon Leung, is a former Google insider who knows all the secrets on using pay per click. Although he is bound by an ironclad nondisclosure agreement, he can still teach the rest of us quite a lot.

GUEST EXPERT ARTICLE

BUILD YOUR LIST WITH PAY PER CLICK

Simon Leung

If you have been around the Internet marketing circuit for a while, I'm sure you understand the importance of building a targeted list of subscribers and customers with whom you can build relationships.

When building your list, one of the most important things to keep in mind is the kind of traffic you are driving to your web site. Ideally, the traffic you get coming to your site should be well targeted visitors. Not only that, but it's always more effective if these visitors proactively sought you out by searching for specific information offered on your web site.

Anyone can send out an e-mail, or ask a partner or colleague to send out an e-mail to another list, and invite someone to check out your web site. But when people have taken it upon themselves to search for a solution to a problem they are experiencing, they are much more likely to give you their name and e-mail address in exchange for that information.

How would you be able to make this happen? The fact is that the answer could very well be right under your nose the entire time!

I'm sure you've heard of Google.com. You may have even used it in your marketing. Did you know that there are thousands of advertisers who are taking advantage of Google's 200 million-plus daily traffic? These advertisers are getting tons of exposure, and many of them are getting highly targeted traffic to their web sites each and every day for just pennies on the dollar! You can do it, too.

You see, Google AdWords is one of the easiest ways to send massive amounts of targeted traffic to your web site instantly and affordably. But you must know how to do it right, because if you set up your AdWords campaign incorrectly, not only could it cost you money on untargeted traffic, but it could also potentially get you penalized by Google.

Google has derived a new set of criteria for web site owners who have list-building objectives in mind. It's not that Google does not allow lead capturing on your web site, but if you do it, you must do so legally, responsibly, and ethically.

One of the most important things when you're setting up your AdWords campaign is to make sure that your keywords are relevant to your business, your ads associated with your keywords are relevant, and the copy on your web site is relevant to your overall AdWords campaign.

Google takes relevance extremely seriously, and relevance often plays the biggest role in determining the quality of your campaign. In addition to having relevant information about your business on your web site, you should also give careful consideration to your list-building strategy.

When capturing your visitors' names and contact information, give them greater peace of mind by providing a link to your official privacy policy, where you have your legal disclaimers that promise not to sell, rent, barter, or share their details, and not to send them any unsolicited, unwanted, and/or irrelevant spam.

In your copy, also give your visitors a preview of what they will receive after giving you their information, such as features and benefits of membership, or a graphic of the product they will receive upon registration. If you do this correctly, and especially if you provide something of value to your visitors (such as an e-book, software, or an e-course) in exchange for their contact information, and also by treating this information responsibly, you will bring in high-quality prospects who are going to love hearing from you!

When you're building your list with Google AdWords, you're receiving visitors who searched on the keywords that you selected and clicked on the ad that you wrote, and you're showing them a solution to a problem about which they are clearly searching. There is no better way to build a large list of targeted subscribers more quickly, easily, and affordably.

So if you're ready to change the way you're doing business online, be sure to start using Google AdWords to build a targeted list today!

(Continued)

> *Simon Leung of http://SimonLeung.com is a former senior AdWords optimization specialist from Google headquarters. Discover his innovative and insider AdWords list-building strategies at http://AdWordsListBuilding.com.*

One of the most successful Internet marketers in the business, and one of the most distinctive, is our friend Wendi Friesen. When you visit Wendi's blog, you'll see someone whose humor and individuality are a big part of her public persona. Wendi sums up her approach in our next guest expert article.

GUEST EXPERT ARTICLE

MADE YOU LOOK!

Wendi Friesen

Internet marketing has come down to one simple concept: Do whatever you can do to make them look!

Hey! This used to be my playground. Being one of the few internet marketers working in the 1990s, I learned to compete for your attention the easy way. Those of us who got in early loved the ease with which we got results from our brainy ideas.

Pay-per-click (PPC) ads were almost foolproof in the beginning. I paid five cents a click and owned most of the keywords in my category. Then came the pleasure seekers. They, too, wanted to find gold in them thar hills, and with the competition for attention and space, we had to start playing by different rules.

It is not enough to be selling online. You've got to make 'em look. And you have to be memorable.

Are You Memorable?

Does your marketing make you unique, interesting, personal, or addictive? Does anything you do have the instant punch? And does it say, "Hey, look at me!"?

I am amazed at how many Web marketers miss the mark. Web sites that have no name, no brand, no picture, and no personality, have no sticking power.

What do you want people to remember?

I don't care who you are or what you are selling, you are going to have to stand out and be memorable. It is still true that all publicity is good publicity, and that it doesn't matter what they say about you, as long as they spell your name right.

Well, most of the time that holds true—and when the publicity is not so good, it is up to you to creatively make it into something wonderful. Internet squabbles are great ways to make you famous. So don't be afraid to make waves. Have an opinion. Get as far away from that middle ground as possible.

As I see it, you have two choices. The first is to sell the same thing everyone else does, in the same way, with the same approach. Don't have an opinion, never offend anyone, take no chances, go only with what is safe, and above all be sure to take the advice of others who will keep you safe.

Or . . . Create your own niche, find your own unique angle, and go nuts with your marketing. Have an opinion. Challenge others. Say things that show your strong opinions. Send out profuse apologies when you screw up. Make people think, make them respond, make them laugh, make them tell their friends.

You might remember that guy on TV with the coat with all those question marks on it—the guy who talked about grants. He has not been on TV for a while, but I still have a picture of him in my mind. He is memorable.

Why? He's a little nuts, different, and screams a lot. The information he offers is pretty much what anyone can get for free. There are certainly more professional sites (like www.GrantMeRich.com, for example). But he's memorable because he's brave, unique, and willing to be nutty.

What will people remember about you? What will make them tell their friends about you? How will you stand out and become addictive?

This is the part that gets a little challenging. If you are a person who loves to play it safe, doesn't make waves, plays by the rules,

(Continued)

only does what all the other sheep do, and would never ever break a rule . . . go get a job. The Internet is not for you.

Here are some ways to make an impact:

- ☞ Ask a question that begs an answer.
- ☞ Get a picture that oozes personality.
- ☞ Challenge your viewers.
- ☞ Create a controversy.
- ☞ Break the rules.

Stop using silly handles when you log into chat rooms, forums, or other interactive Internet places. Use your full name. If you want people to remember you, don't miss an opportunity to put your *real name* in front of them.

Be generous. Give your readers something they didn't expect. Go above and beyond what they expect, and know that your generosity will create more goodwill and loyalty than just about anything else you might do. The worst that will happen when you take a marketing risk is that people will remember you for the silly marketing thing you did.

Being a hypnotist, I like the idea of going overboard with the hypnosis angle. I let people know that when I snap my fingers they will be in my power. When I snap, they listen.

I let my followers know that I am willing to hypnotize them against their will and use them as part of my plot to take over the world. On my weekly radio show, I tell my listeners that I will do my best to get them dancing naked on the tables, going to the bank and withdrawing all their money, and making my every wish their instant command.

So here it is, my *SNAP* formula to remember when you are deciding on a marketing approach or a new campaign, or even when you are making a new web page:

S is for *splash*. Make a big splash. *Shock* them, *surprise* them, tell them a *secret* about you.

N is for *niche*. Create a niche that doesn't exist. *Nag* your readers until they realize they can't live without you. Toss in a little *nookie!* Be flirty and playful and sexy in your approach.

A is for *addicting* your readers. Create a personality that becomes an addiction and keeps 'em coming back for more. *Ask* them questions that make them think. Give them more than they expected. Make them interact with you so they have to pay *attention* to you for the *answers*.

P is for *personality*. You have to find your own unique self. The Internet doesn't need another boring web site or e-mail. *Punch* it up! Find out what makes you *powerful*. *Please* your reader and visitors with your unusual style and charm and be as weird as you can be.

And what have I done to make my business SNAP? I love to make videos. My staff dressed me in a straightjacket and I escaped. I told dirty jokes to the camera.

I ate a lemon. And much more. I trust you will be enjoying it soon at http://wendi.blip.tv.

And now I will let you in on my most brilliant marketing moment in the history of everything. I asked my customers to record a testimonial on their phone that is about one of my products. The best one, most creative and unique, would get $500. The next week, my customers were all asked to listen to, and vote for, the best and most creative one. Brilliant, I know.

Find a nutty idea, go for it, and in everything you do, make 'em look!

Wendi Friesen, CHT, operates the number one hypnosis web site on the Internet, www.Wendi.com, rated by Alexa.com. She is a popular speaker for corporations, sales teams, medical professionals, and athletes. Wendi hosts her own radio show, www.WendiRadio.com, and has appeared in numerous television programs and publications.

Resource Page

Summary of topics discussed in this chapter:
- ☞ E-mail marketing.
- ☞ Articles.
- ☞ Search engine optimization.
- ☞ Your blog.
- ☞ Branding.
- ☞ Joint ventures.
- ☞ Your affiliate program.
- ☞ Newsletters.
- ☞ Newsgroups.
- ☞ Press releases and public relations.
- ☞ Teleseminars.
- ☞ Audio and video recordings.
- ☞ Viral products.
- ☞ Rebrandable products.
- ☞ Cross promotions.
- ☞ Your own forum.
- ☞ Giving testimonials.
- ☞ Buying or trading advertising.
- ☞ Exit traffic.
- ☞ Offers to unsubscribers.
- ☞ Free reports tied to keywords.
- ☞ Pay per click.

In this chapter, guest expert Annie Jennings writes about using public relations; Jim Edwards discusses webinars; Simon Leung writes about how to use pay-per-click advertising; and Wendi Friesen talks about the art of self-promotion.

Go to www.YourInternetCashMachine.com and find a treasure trove of resources to help you promote your Internet business, as well as interviews with our guest experts. Claim your free membership now!

MAKE IT HYPNOTIC!

As you will read shortly, Joe has been fascinated by hypnotism since childhood. When he became a writer and a marketer, he began to look at writing sales copy in terms of hypnosis. Over the years, he has written extensively on the subject of *hypnotic writing*, and has trained many top Internet marketers, including Jillian, in his methods. We are sharing the basis of his ideas with you here, and we encourage you to adopt these principles as you write your own sales copy.

How many web sites do you visit a day? If you're like most surfers, you probably visit a dozen or more. Depending on how much time you have, or whether you're under 20 years old, you might even visit hundreds of sites a day.

Now here's the million-dollar question: How many times do you sign up for a newsletter or buy something as a result of visiting those sites?

My guess is, not many—certainly not at all of them.

Well, why not? Why did you visit the site and leave without taking action? Why didn't you sign up for the newsletter, or download anything, or buy something right then and there? Oh, you may have bookmarked the page for later viewing. But we all know few of us ever return to those bookmarked pages. Why is that?

The truth is, most web sites don't do the job for which they were designed. People are spending far too much time trying to make their web sites pretty. They add graphics, sound, and even video, all designed to dazzle the visitor. The thing is, those bells and whistles don't inspire action.

What *does* cause action? What does cause people to sign up for a newsletter, or download a freebie, or actually part with their money and buy something online? It can be answered in two words: *hypnotic writing*.

Few could have predicted it ten years ago, but writing is the sales engine online. Words are what cause people to take action. Without words, people are left wondering what to do. Even experienced web designers are admitting this fact.

"My company has helped create about 10,000 web sites so far," a web designer told Joe recently. He went on to confess, "I can create web sites and I can teach people to create web sites and I can even drive traffic to web sites, but if you don't have words on those sites that persuade, then you won't convert a single visitor into a single buyer. Those sites will be worthless."

We agree. But just in case you need further convincing, try this experiment for yourself: Build a web site with no words. Use all the graphics, sound, and video you like, but don't use any words at all on the site. Then watch what happens. You might get some people taking action simply out of curiosity, but you won't get the results you want without words. Words motivate. Words sell. Words rule.

As Freud said in 1915, "Words were originally magic and to this day words have retained much of their ancient magical power."

Of course, these can't be just any words. Words for words' sake is what we call a dictionary. That's boring. You need words combined in such a way that they get attention, hold it, and cause action. Those kinds of words are hard to come by, but not all that difficult to create. Again, it's called hypnotic writing. And that's what we teach you in this chapter. By the time you finish reading this, you will feel confident in creating your own hypnotic writing on your own web site.

Imagine what your life will be like when your web site not only gets traffic, but gets people taking action, too! Are you ready?

WHAT IS HYPNOTIC WRITING?

Recently Joe spoke at the world's largest hypnosis convention. Professional hypnotists from all over the world came to hear him describe hypnotic writing. He told the crowd that hypnotic writing creates a form of *waking hypnosis*. This is not magical or mystical. It's no different than being absorbed in a good movie or riveted by a good book, or driving down the highway for hours and being zoned out. In each instance you are in a form of waking trance.

In 1956 an anonymous hypnotist, writing in his famous mail-order course, *Dynamic Speed Hypnosis,* declared: "Anything you do which makes your listeners react because of *mental images* you plant in their minds is *waking hypnosis!*"

Just replace "listeners" with "readers" and "waking hypnosis" with "hypnotic writing" in the sentence you just read and you have a good working definition of hypnotic writing. It would read like this: "Anything you do which makes your readers react because of *mental images* you plant in their minds is *hypnotic writing!*"

Again, hypnotic writing induces a form of *waking hypnosis*. It is characterized by a focus of attention. It is a trance state in which you are wide awake but focused on something you are reading. Hypnotic writing achieves this state by the right use of words to create mental experiences. In other words, you get people so interested in your web site that almost nothing else matters. And if you do this right, your hypnotic writing will lead your visitors to take action.

All of this will make sense as we walk you through the steps of how to create hypnotic writing. When you do so, people will visit your site and actually *do* something as a result. What will they do? That's up to you. If you want them to sign up for your newsletter, they'll do it. If you want them to download something, they will. If you want them to buy, they will do that, too.

How? With hypnotic writing. Why? Because hypnotic writing activates the unconscious mind in people.

Let us show you a simple way to make this happen.

THE FORMULA FOR CAUSING ACTION

As you probably already know, there are two ways to cause people to take action. One is pain and the other is pleasure. These have been known throughout history as the two primary human activators. In short, you can get people to move either with a board smacked across their butt or with a juicy carrot dangling in front of their face.

Most people in marketing and psychology agree that the first motivator—pain—is more powerful than the second. While we agree, we think that is a disservice to mankind. Why add to the misery in the world? Instead, let's make a difference and focus on pleasure. Let's make people happy. We think that is a sounder way to help people, as well as help yourself. Can you imagine how wonderful life would be for all of us if we focused on our wants—our desires, our pleasures, our goals—and not our pains?

But let's start with the basic formula for persuading people, which traditionally includes the pain motivator. Starting here will give you a better sense of how to use Joe's revised system later on your own web site, which we'll explain in a moment. This four-step strategy is probably 2,500 years old, and goes back to Aristotle and the ancient Greeks. In short, and in a very simplified version, here it is:

1. Problem
2. Promise
3. Proof
4. Price

Not much to it, is there? Let's look at each step and see.

Problem

Begin your web site with a headline that calls out the audience you want by focusing on their problem. For example, if you sell something to cure, say, heel spurs, than use a headline such as "Got heel spurs?" Or say you are selling a weight-loss product of some sort. You might use a headline such as "Want to lose weight?"

What you are doing is rounding up the people who will want to buy from you by focusing on their problem or issue. In other words, you created a web site and you're getting traffic there, but unless you use hypnotic writing to grab attention, hold it, and lead it to action, then forget it—your site is a loser.

Again, say you are a massage therapist with your own site. Your headline at the top of your web site might be "Stressed? Want to release your tension in 30 minutes or less?"

By now you should grasp what we're doing here. We're simply suggesting you ask yourself, "What is the problem my visitors are having?" Whatever it is, you create a lead headline at the top of your web site that speaks to it.

Promise

You got their attention with step one. Now mention your promise. Using the "heel spurs" headline from earlier, a follow-through might be "New herbs reduce or remove heel spurs in 30 days." The second example, on losing weight, might read "New nondiet approach relies on your mind, not your food, to lose weight fast." And the massage therapist example might read "My hands have eased 3,500 bodies just like yours. I can help you, too."

As you can probably gather, what you are doing in this second step is explaining how you solve the problem mentioned in the first step. This will keep people reading. If you truly focus on their problem, you will be putting them into a waking trance with hypnotic writing.

Proof

Next, you need proof. We live in the age of skepticism. People are used to going to web sites and hearing wild or unsubstantiated claims. Their guard is up. Not only that, but in the United States, the Federal Trade Commission (FTC) is watching you. They want proof, too, that you can deliver.

So step three in this formula is to focus on your proof, or your evidence. This can be in the form of a guarantee, testimonials, or anything else you can think of to convince people you are being honest with them. Some examples might be "Your heel spurs will disappear in 30 days or you can have all your money back"; "Over 11,500 people healed of heel spurs so far"; "Research shows people lose an average of 33 pounds with this new plan"; "You will feel so relaxed from my massage that you will fall asleep on my table."

And so it goes. Again, what you are doing is proving your promise. This is where you bring in your evidence that your promise will work.

Price

Finally, you need to ask for what you want. If you want people to sign up for your newsletter, say so. If you want them to buy your product, say so. If you want them to call you, say so. People want to be led. But they won't take action unless you spell it out for them and tell them the price for doing so. Examples might be "If you don't take care of those heel spurs today, where will you be tomorrow?" "Order our special herbs right now for only $19.95."

THE UPDATED FORMULA

Philosopher Vernon Howard once said, "If we believe in the necessity of trying to win over others, we will also believe in the need for wearisome scheming."

Let's not scheme. Let's not try to win people over to our web sites. Instead, let's focus on what *they* want. Let's focus on their pleasure, not their pain. The more you can deliver the good that people long for, the more people will almost hypnotically be drawn to you and your website.

Remember, we said we don't think we need to add to the bleakness of the world. So we're going to be bold and say let's delete step one altogether.

If you focus on pain, you surely get people's attention. You are speaking to their greatest concern. Have you noticed how often ads on television and in newspapers focus on pain to get your attention? The method works. But we don't want to add to the pain in the world. Since a basic truth in psychology is that people get more of whatever they focus on, we don't even want to mention the pain. So let's try creating a basic hypnotic message with just the other three steps:

1. Promise
2. Proof
3. Price

Here's how it might work. In step one, you round up your audience by focusing on what they want. An example might be "Want to play the guitar fast and easy?" You then go to step two and offer proof.

For example, "Amy's Stripped Down Guitar Method promises to teach you how to play your favorite song in one weekend flat." Finally, in step three, you ask for their order by mentioning the price: "For only $19.99, you can be playing the guitar at the end of this weekend. Just click here . . ."

There you have it. You created a basic hypnotically written message and didn't cause people to feel bad at all. Your final piece of writing might look like this: "Want to play the guitar in one weekend flat? Amy's Stripped Down Guitar Method e-book shows anyone how to do it, guaranteed or your money back. Click here to pay $19.99 and download it right now."

Not bad for a few minutes work. But is that good enough for your web site?

And how do you apply this to your website, anyway? Just keep reading . . .

WHAT ABOUT YOUR WEB SITE?

You're intelligent enough to know the preceding formula will help you easily create a short piece of very simple hypnotic writing. That might be fine for an ad, a postcard, a telegram, or of course an e-mail. But what about a full-scale web site? How do you apply Joe's three-step hypnotic formula to create your own hypnotically written web site?

The answer should be obvious—it's certainly simple. All you do is expand on each of the three steps in this peace-loving formula. In other words:

1. Promise. Your headline can be short and sweet. But why not a secondary headline under it? That works, too.
2. Proof. Your proof can be testimonials, a guarantee, scientific studies, quotes from authorities, a statistic, or anything else that helps convince people of your promise.
3. Price. Your call to action can be several reminders to buy now, as well as how to buy, where to buy, and when to buy. You want people to act now, not tomorrow, so your price might include bonuses for acting right this minute, such as "Order now and get three e-books for free."

You can see an example of how the three steps have been used to create a full-blown web site at http://www.strippeddownguitar.com/. We're using it as a model because Joe knows the author of the site and helped her create it. If you look at the site closely, you'll find she uses longer copy to expand on each of the three points in the formula. Let's look at some excerpts.

The *promise* is conveyed through a headline that says

How to play any song you love on the guitar—in one weekend flat!

followed by an expansion of this in a subheading:

Find out how to amaze your friends, your loved ones, and most of all, yourself by singing and playing songs you love in as little as one weekend—even if you've never touched a guitar before, are tone deaf, and suffer from major stage fright!

The next portion of the web site offers the *proof*:

I promise, after just one weekend with Stripped-Down Guitar, you will be inspired and thrilled with how satisfying the guitar can be! And once you've gotten a taste of impressing your friends and family by performing your favorite songs, you will be completely stoked!

"Playing guitar Stripped-Down style is clear, concise, and geared to give you quick results that will keep you engaged and excited about your developing skills.

"In Stripped-Down Guitar, I reveal secrets like:

- ☞ *My one-weekend, step-by-step "stripped-down" method to start playing the guitar.*
- ☞ *The two guitar accessories a beginner cannot do without.*
- ☞ *The best place to find the chords to your favorite songs on the Internet.*
- ☞ *The most important secret to choosing your first song to learn.*
- ☞ *Finger by finger instructions for making the most common guitar chords.*

☛ *The indispensable secret for actually getting your fingers to learn faster.*

☛ *The number one thing you need to know about guitar tab sites that I had to learn the very hard way.*

☛ *The most important technique for freeing up space in your brain to learn more quickly.*

☛ *The little-known fact that can make a decent singer out of anyone and the one secret that can have you singing any song better . . . instantly!*

☛ *The four indispensable techniques for overcoming stage fright.*

☛ *How to deal with an unsympathetic audience member.*

. . . so you can capture the magic of being a musician, even if you never dreamed you could!

Lastly, the *price* is conveyed in a clear, reassuring manner, offering enticing guarantees and overcoming all potential objections or concerns.

Click to order Stripped-Down Guitar *now!*

Your satisfaction is assured through our no-risk, you-can't-lose, 100 percent, no-questions-asked, iron-clad money-back guarantee.

If for any reason, you aren't thrilled and satisfied with your purchase, just contact me directly within 30 days and I'll refund 100 percent of your purchase price.

What I'm saying is don't decide now if Stripped-Down Guitar *is right for you.*

Try it out for one full month—risk free.

If it doesn't help you overcome any stumbling blocks to learning to play great songs on the guitar; if it doesn't guide you step-by-step through picking a song, learning it, and honing it for performance; if it doesn't take you by the hand and teach you exactly how to get your fingers working and how to get your voice out there—even if you've been labeled "tone deaf" or never thought you could play; if it doesn't make progress on guitar easier than you ever dreamed possible; and if it doesn't inspire you to keep on learning and playing, then I don't want your money . . . and I'll gladly give it all back.

You have nothing to lose!

So how much is this tremendous experience going to cost you? Well, the regular price for Stripped-Down Guitar *is $39.99. However, for a limited time, we are running an introductory offer and you can have it at a discount for only $19.99. That's 50 percent off—but you must* act now!

Plus, because you download *the course, you can have this information immediately, and get started learning to play the guitar today! And it doesn't matter if it's 2:00 in the morning!*

Click to order Stripped-Down Guitar *now!*

Amy successfully covered all three steps in Joe's formula—promise, proof, and price—with words that are easy to read. If you are at all interested in learning how to play the guitar fast, you'll buy Amy's e-book.

But how much copy on your web site is too much?

HOW LONG IS TOO LONG?

By now you can see that you can make your web site pretty lengthy just following the three-step formula. This doesn't mean you want a web site that runs on forever. But it does mean you can take your time to share your message. After all, people will read any amount of words on a web site, as long as they are *interesting to them.* And that's the trick that makes millionaires out of paupers.

Keep in mind that as a general rule, *the more you tell, the more you sell.* That means, don't be afraid of long copy (*copy* means *words* in marketing lingo). Web sites with long copy (lots of words) tend to do better than web sites with fewer words. But again, they can't be just any words. As you know, if you bore people, they will leave your site in a nanosecond.

Our own rule of thumb is this: *The more money you are asking for, the more words you should write.*

If you are only asking people to sign up for a free newsletter, a few well-chosen words may do. If you want them to buy something under $10, again, a few well-chosen words may be enough. But if you want someone to buy a $15,000 exercise machine—as the people at http://www.FastExercise.com want you to do—you have a lot of explaining to do. That will take some words. They'd better be hypnotic words, too.

The point is, the length of copy at your web site will depend on what you are selling. If people are familiar with your product or service, you may not have to say much. If people easily understand why your price is what it is, again, you may not have to say much. But if you have to explain your product, or your price, do so with as many words as you need.

Your guiding principle should always be to focus on the interests of the people visiting your site. Again, people are willing to read long copy—they read books, articles, and newspapers, for example—as long as it is interesting *to them*. If people aren't reading your web site copy, then you haven't written to *their* interests.

Let's take a closer look at how to interest people.

HOW PEOPLE THINK

As we mentioned earlier, the average web site is terrible. Most web sites are written by people talking about themselves and begging you to buy from them. In order for you to be different, you'll need to write the way people think. You'll need to create hypnotic writing in our favorite of all forms: the story.

Once upon a time Roger Schank, writing in his thought-provoking, scholarly book, *Tell Me A Story* (Northwestern University Press, 1995), stated, "We do not easily remember what other people have said if they do not tell it in the form of a story. We can learn from the stories of others, but only if what we hear relates strongly to something we already knew." Elsewhere he writes, "People think in terms of stories."

In short, if you want to create hypnotic writing on your web site that follows the basic three-step formula we've taught you, then the best form is through a story.

We love stories. The most successful articles, books, web sites, and even audio packages, all include stories. Stories are a powerful way to get your message across. People don't usually defend against a story. And, as Schank pointed out, people actually *think* in stories.

If you remember the definition we gave earlier—"Anything you do which makes your listeners react because of *mental images* you plant in their minds is *waking hypnosis!*"—then you can easily see that written stories are a terrific way to create mental images that lead to a waking trance stance.

When people read your story, it takes place in their head. This is a powerful place for you to be. You are in a person's operating control panel. The more you cause them to think in terms of mental images, the closer you get to causing them to take action at your web site. In short, stories are a potent tool.

But how do you create a story composed of hypnotic writing that actually moves people to action? Let's look at that next.

HOW TO CREATE HYPNOTIC STORIES

This is easier than you might think. What you want to do is remember a true story of something that happened as a result of someone using your product or service. It needs to be true because, again, we're trying to spread honesty and goodwill across the Internet. It also needs to be true so the FTC doesn't jump on you for fabrications in your promise. And finally, if it's true, it's easier to write.

For example, Joe recently recorded Dr. Robert Anthony's powerful material, *Beyond Positive Thinking*, which Joe thinks is the holy grail of self-improvement wisdom. When Joe was creating the web site to promote the CD set (which you can see at http://www.BeyondPositive Thinking.com), he asked Dr. Anthony to give him a few stories of how people used his famous material to get results in their life. One of the stories Dr. Anthony gave Joe is now on the site (and is used with Dr. Anthony's permission). Here it is.

The Story of Ramon

by Dr. Robert Anthony

Many years ago I met a man named Ramon. In fact, I dedicated an entire chapter to him in my book Doing What You Love—Loving What You Do *(Berkley Trade, 1991). Ramon is one of the most successful businessmen in California as well as one of the most spiritually evolved beings I have ever met.*

I met Ramon because a friend had given him a copy of Beyond Positive Thinking. *Ramon buys every self-improvement tape album sold. He has all of Nightingale-Conant's products, plus more. He never plays the radio in his Rolls Royce. Instead, he listens to personal development programs on his 60-minute ride to and from his office—even though he is already a successful multi-millionaire.*

Ramon told me, "Your Beyond Positive Thinking *recordings are the best ever produced by anyone. I should know, I own all of them!" He was so impressed at how they could help other people, he would buy 25 sets at a time and put them in the trunk of his Rolls Royce. Anytime he met someone who he felt needed help, he would give them a set free of charge. He frequently called me to tell me of the "miraculous" results they had with the tapes and how it changed their lives.*

Over the years he bought over 300 sets from me, and to this day he says that he has never found anything more powerful to change lives than Beyond Positive Thinking.

As you can see, that story silently communicates an almost hypnotic message: *Dr. Robert Anthony's recordings work.*

Had we just come out and said "Dr. Robert Anthony's methods work," you could dismiss the thought. You might think we are just trying to sell you something. But when someone else proves the statement, without actually saying it, through a captivating story, then the message goes right into people's unconscious minds. You slipped in past their mental radar.

Of course, someplace on your web site you might declare "Dr. Robert Anthony's methods work." That's fine. Declarations can be hypnotic, too. That's why hypnotists say, "You are getting sleepier and sleepier" and not "Are you getting sleepy yet?" Commands work. But what we are advising you to do here is to *also* create a story that conveys the same message. This way you are speaking to people's conscious as well as subconscious minds.

Stories are powerful for another reason, too. The following section might be considered advanced hypnotic writing, but we want to discuss it to give you a sense of the power you hold in your hands when you create a web site with hypnotic stories and hypnotic writing.

REMINDERS AS TRIGGERS

Have you ever truly analyzed a conversation?

What typically happens is someone talks to you about an event in their life. They are sharing their story. That's simple enough. But what happens next is you look through your memory banks for something similar to what you just heard. You might say, "Something like that happened to me once, too!" And then you take your turn in the conversation. As the person listens to you, they are doing the same thing. They might even get so excited when a thought or memory occurs to them that they interrupt you and tell their next story.

What is happening here?

Roger Schank, writing in *Tell Me A Story*, says, "The question to think about is how, after someone says something to you in conversation, something comes to mind to say back. Even the simplest of responses have to be found somewhere in memory."

In short, stories contain elements—usually specific words—that trigger memories in people. When Joe tells you about his experience of having lunch today, and mentions that an attractive young blonde-haired woman waited on him and seemed to flirt with him, he is setting you up to drift off, mentally, from the conversation. The word *lunch* might remind you that you haven't eaten yet, and now suddenly you're thinking about food. Or his mention of the attractive young woman might remind you of sex, and suddenly your mind is off someplace entirely different.

Where *did* your mind go, anyway?

Again, stories contain triggers. Schank calls them *reminders*. These triggers are reminders of previous thoughts. These triggers will cause people to mentally drift into an imagery experience that may or may not serve you. If you want people thinking about food, mention lunch. If you want people thinking about sex, mention the attractive young woman. But also be aware of what is happening here. Your words are causing activity in the other person's mind.

This is what happens when anyone has a conversation. One sentence said by one person leads to a reminder in the other person, which leads to their saying something. The next person then hears a reminder, and makes their follow-up statement. Two people in rapport and talking a mile a minute are two people experiencing reminders.

All of this is good news for you and your web site. You want to consciously control your visitor's mental experience through your hypnotic writing. Again, use stories to convey your message. But keep in mind that the words you use within those stories will trigger reminders. You want people thinking of you and your site in a positive way, so refrain from any negative reminders. Keep people focused on what they get from your product or service, and keep them focused with a story that reminds them of their wants.

As you read this, you will start to remember stories that have influenced you. But let us show you a longer example right now. This is an article that demonstrates how Joe used a story to make a point and then lead people to what he wanted them to learn. Notice how the story beginning this article helps prove the fact that hypnosis is real.

GUEST EXPERT ARTICLE

BUYING TRANCES: THE REAL SECRET TO HYPNOTIC SELLING

Dr. Joe Vitale

I couldn't snap Billy out of his trance.

It happened over 30 years ago. I was a teenager fascinated by the powers of the mind. I read about spirituality, psychic phenomena, UFOs, past lives, present problems, the magic of believing, and yes, even hypnosis.

And that helps explain why I had my best friend, Billy, in a deep trance in the basement of my parent's home in Ohio. I had regressed him from the age of 16 back to the age of 4 or 5. I had no business doing it. But I was curious and Billy was game.

It was a remarkable morning until something truly terrifying happened.

I snapped my fingers—the prearranged command to wake Billy up—but he stayed in the chair, smiling, eyes closed, and laughing loud and hard.

(Continued)

"How old are you?" I asked, wanting to check his age level.

"Seventy-two, how old are you?!" he replied, laughing like a wild, untamed, truly obnoxious child.

You can't imagine my fear.

"When I slap my hands together, you will awaken," I commanded. Billy laughed long and loud. I slapped my hands together. Billy laughed louder and longer.

I'm panicking now. I'm barely 16 years old. I have my best friend in a trance, regressed to a young age, and I can't bring him out of it. I could see my parent's rage. I could see Billy's parents' rage. I could see myself locked up, still a teenager, all because I practiced hypnosis like other kids played baseball or monopoly.

I waited. I held my breath. I snapped my fingers. I slapped my hands. I perspired. Billy wasn't coming out of his trance. He was locked into another time period. And I was responsible.

Some kids borrow the neighbor's car and wreck it. I borrowed my best friend's mind and put it in park.

What was I going to do?

I don't recall how much time went by before I decided to call for help. I remember going to the phone book and desperately searching for a hypnotist to call for help. I found one in Cleveland, Ohio, a hundred miles from my home. I called him, got him on the phone, and acted as cool as I could.

"Doctor, my name is Joe, and, well, I've been learning about hypnosis. I was just wondering, what would happen if you put someone in a trance and they, well, er, ah, you know, never came out of it?"

There was silence on the line.

Then I remember the voice bellowing at me.

"Are you practicing hypnosis there?!"

"Oh, no," I lied. "I was just curious what would happen if, you know, you put your best friend under, regressed him, and he wouldn't come out of it. Is that a bad thing?"

"Is your best friend there now?"

The hypnotist was on to me.

"Well . . . yes."

"Will he come to the phone?"

"He won't do *anything* I ask," I said. My voice was cracking now. I was scared and it showed.

"Don't worry about it," the hypnotist advised me. "He'll either naturally awaken shortly, or he'll fall asleep and then wake up."

"But he thinks he's five years old," I added.

"You kids have to stop playing around!" he roared.

"But I want to be a hypnotist someday," I explained.

"Get training first!" he blurted.

"Okay, okay, I will," I said. "But what do I do about Billy?"

"Put him on the phone."

I went to Billy, somehow got him to get on the phone, and the hypnotist said something that helped Billy awaken. To this day I don't know what he said. And since I haven't seen Billy in nearly 20 years, I have no idea how old Billy really thinks he is. I understand he's now a state trooper in Ohio, so I imagine he's stable and well. Still, I'm staying in Texas.

Buying Trances

I learned something profound that day in my parent's basement when my life stopped for an afternoon. I learned that trances are powerful. They are real. And we are all in them.

That's right. You're in a trance. Yes, right now. So am I. We may not think we're five years old, but we think we are writers, or marketers, or salespeople, or some other trance. As long as we believe the trance we are in, we will play it out perfectly. When we wake up, we'll just be in another trance. Even the "I'm now awake" trance is just another trance.

Stay with me here. Whether you disagree or not, there's a valuable lesson here, one that can help you increase your sales and your profits.

In short, your prospects are all in trances. If you merge with their trance, you can then lead them out of it and into the buying trance you want them to be in.

I'll repeat that: Your prospects are all in trances. If you merge with their trance, you can then lead them out of it and into the buying trance you want them to be in.

Let me explain with an example. Say you want to sell a new software program that helps people incorporate their business.

(Continued)

How would you do it? The average person might send out a sales letter that says, "New program makes incorporating a snap." That approach would get some sales, especially from people already wanting to incorporate.

But a more hypnotic approach would be to run a headline such as this: "Tired of paying too much in taxes? Read this surprising way out of the maze!" This approach would merge with the existing trance in many businesspeople. In other words, they are in the "taxes suck" trance and the "small businesses get screwed" trance. Agree with them. Merge with them. Accept that trance as your door. Then lead into what you want to sell by tying it back to their trance.

Let's break down this process into three steps:

1. What do your prospects believe right now? (Current trance.)
2. Agree with their beliefs to merge with them. (Rapport.)
3. Lead their beliefs into your offer. (New trance.)

That's it. That's the real secret to hypnotic selling.

Let's take another example. Say you want to sell a pair of pants. How would you use our hypnotic selling, three-step process to move them?

1. What do your prospects believe right now about pants? A little research would help. Let's say they believe all pants are the same. They are in the "all pants are alike" trance. That's their current trance, or mind-set. You would not be very wise to argue with it. Instead, accept it and go to step two.
2. Agree with them. In person, on the phone, or in your headlines, say something that lets your prospects know you are in the same trance. Use statements such as "I thought all pants were alike, too," or "No pants are different—so why even look at this pair?" This creates rapport. You can't sell to anyone without creating rapport. So step two is a way to meet people where they are. Consciously join their unconscious trance. Then go to the next step.
3. Now lead them into your offer. You might say something like, "Why are people saying these pants are different? Here's why." This is taking them into a new trance, a trance that says "Some

pants are different"—a buying trance. Because you acknowledged the trance they were in, and merged with them, you are now in position—a very powerful position—to sell them.

There are numerous ways to find people's trances, merge with them, and then lead them into a "buy from you" trance. I can't discuss all of them in this short article—I'm just giving you the tip of the iceberg here. But before I end, let's look at some existing trances your prospects may be in when you call or send them a sales piece. They include:

- ☛ "I'm worried about money" trance.
- ☛ "I'm lonely" trance.
- ☛ "I'm afraid of people" trance.
- ☛ "I'm sick and tired of my job" trance.
- ☛ "I'm fed up with my kids" trance.
- ☛ "The world sucks" trance.
- ☛ "I'm hungry" trance.
- ☛ "I need to lose weight" trance.

And so it goes. You'll notice that each of these trances is self-serving. That's the nature of people. They are interested in their well-being first. They are preoccupied with their own needs, desires, pains, and more.

Any inward state is a trance. Naturally, everyone is in one trance or another when you call them or write them. Your job is to note it, merge with it, and lead them out of it.

Here's one final example to make this process clearer for you. Let's say you want to sell a music recording. We'll make it a classical CD. Follow these steps:

1. What trance are people already in? You can imagine they come home from work, find your sales letter in their mail, and are *not* in the mood for it. Your headline might say, "Just got home from work?"
2. Create rapport by acknowledging their trance. You might write, "Since you just got home from work, are probably tired

(Continued)

and ready to toss this mail in the trash, wait one second before you do it."

3. Now introduce your new trance. Maybe write: "Imagine putting a CD on that fills your mind with soothing, relaxing, healing music . . . the kind of heavenly sound that helps drift far, far away from your day . . ."

To end this article, let me remind you of what Billy taught me when I was a kid: Everyone is in a trance and everyone can be brought out of it. The idea is not to ignore this quirk of human nature, but to use it for the well-being of all you touch—including your own profit.

Just don't age-regress any of your prospects!

Joe's article proves that stories can be the finest form of hypnotic writing you'll ever put on your web site. So look for stories. Record them. Write them down. And add them to your site to bring it to life with hypnotic writing.

But what about just transforming your existing web copy into hypnotic writing? How do you take your existing sentences and add to them or actually rewrite them to give them more power? How do you do *that*?

Well, let's see . . .

CHANGING AVERAGE WRITING INTO HYPNOTIC WRITING

Let us tell you a secret. Whenever someone hires Joe to rewrite their website, he runs a "copy translation service" in his head. What he does is read each sentence of their site as though it were written in a foreign language. The foreign language is *ego copy*. It was written by the person who owns the site and is usually full of fluff. What Joe does is translate that ego copy into *reader copy*. That means he takes their line and turns it into a line that speaks to the visitor's interest.

An example might help. Nearly every site you visit will contain a "we" statement. It's usually something like, "We have been in business five years" or "We love to make donuts" (or whatever they make). All of those are ego copy statements. That's a foreign language to your readers. It doesn't appeal to your reader at all.

Joe translates those ego statements into reader benefits or reader copy. He might turn "We have been in business five years" to "You can rest assured you will get your item from us on time and to your satisfaction, as we've been doing this for over five years." And he might turn "We love to make donuts" to "You'll love our mouth-watering donuts because our passion for making them energizes every one we create for you."

Do you see the difference? Most sites focus on the person who created the site. What you want to focus on is the interests of the person visiting your site. In short, get out of your ego and into the visitor's ego. Speak to *their* interests.

We do not have enough space here to fully teach you how to transform your web site into hypnotic writing. Joe has written plenty of books to help you there. (See http://www.MrFire.com for a complete catalog of his work.) But let's look at some basic tips. The following are excerpts from Joe's e-book, *The Hypnotic Writing Swipe File*, which you can learn more about at http://www.HypnoticWritingSwipeFile.com.

Hypnotic Headline Words

You can generate headlines for your web site fast simply by using words from the following list. Simply add them to your product or service, claim or guarantee, and watch how easy it is to write a hypnotic headline.

announcing	initial	super
astonishing	improved	time-sensitive
at last	love	unique
exciting	limited	urgent
exclusive	offer	wonderful
fantastic	powerful	you
fascinating	phenomenal	breakthrough
first	revealing	introducing
free	revolutionary	new
guaranteed	special	how-to
incredible	successful	

For example, "Announcing: Astonishing guaranteed free new way to find love now!"

Since we're on the subject of headlines, marketing gurus have found that when they remove the banner at the top of their web site, they often get twice as many sales. Get that: *Twice as many sales!* Why? It seems that the banner distracts from what really does the engaging and the selling: the headline.

Again, what sells online—what motivates people to take action—are words.

Hypnotic Openings

These will easily help you start any writing almost without thinking. They are prompters, mind joggers, and brain stimuli. Just read them and fill in the blank with whatever comes to mind. For example, in your opening sentence, tell your readers what they will learn or what feelings they will get from reading your web site.

> As you start reading this article you find yourself . . .
> As you sit there and read the beginning of this report you start to feel . . .
> As you read every word of this report you will become (amazed, stunned, etc.) at . . .
> As you analyze each word of this document you will shortly feel a sense of . . . (calmness, joy, etc.).
> As you scan every word of this web page you will begin to discover new ways of . . .
> After you read this short article, you will feel . . .
> Can you imagine . . .
> Picture yourself five years from now . . .
> Just picture . . .
> Just imagine . . .
> Remember when you were in high school . . .
> Imagine what it would be like if . . .
> Wouldn't it be amazing if . . .
> And in those early years of existence . . .
> Imagine what it would be like if you could . . .
> See yourself . . .

Remember the smell of . . .
And you begin to notice . . .
Do you remember hearing . . .
Can you recall what a (insert word) feels like?

Tip: Use statements at the beginning of your writing that your prospects already know to be true. This creates trust right away. Trust leads to sales—and to getting people to do anything else you may want them to do. For example:

You probably know . . .
You're intelligent enough to know . . .
Of course you've heard that . . .
Everyone knows . . .
You probably already know this . . .
Rare thinking people like you already know that . . .

Psychological Copy Connectors

Copy connectors are ways to weave your sentences and paragraphs together to end up with a web site that compels people to take the actions you want.

Tell your readers what they're thinking or feeling as they read your words. Most people will actually start thinking or feeling it because you brought it up. Only induce thoughts that will attract them to buy your product.

What if you . . .
Little by little you begin . . .
And as you absorb this information, you'll . . .
And as you are thinking about . . ., you become really interested . . .
Are you beginning to see how . . .
As you read each word in this letter, . . .
Have you noticed yet that . . .
Now I would like to help you experience . . .
Wouldn't it be amazing if . . .
And you will sink deeper and deeper . . .

And you will start to feel better and better about . . .
The further and further you browse toward the end of this report,
    slowly your problem . . .

Using the Tips

As you can imagine, how you use the preceding tips is up to you. But
let us give you some pointers. For example, you might have a line on
your site that says, "My e-product gets results." You could rewrite that
to say, "The further and further you read into this web site, the more
you will realize that my e-product gets results." See the difference?

The first line—"My e-product gets results"—is bland. The average
web site contains that kind of limp writing.

The second line—"The further and further you read into this web
site, the more you will realize that my e-product gets results"—is hypnotic writing. It conveys a command and an assumption. Combined,
they help lead to action.

Go through your web site with these ideas in mind. Look for
places to rewrite, add phrases, or in any other way grab and hold your
visitors' attention. Remember, to create hypnotic writing, you have to
focus on the interests of your visitors, not yourself.

Hypnotic Quiz

Would you like to have a little fun right now? Here's a brief quiz to
help you realize how easy it is to add the preceding phrases and
sentence starters to your writing. Go back through this section and see
if you can spot all the times we slipped in a hypnotic phrase.

Wouldn't it be amazing if you spotted every time we put a hypnotic twist on a sentence?

Clue: "Wouldn't it be amazing" is a phrase from the preceding list.

You probably know that we've used hypnotic writing throughout
this article.

"You probably know" is also a phrase from this collection. Are you
beginning to see how easy this is?

"Are you beginning to see how" is also from this collection of
phrases!

FINAL THOUGHTS

By now you probably understand that the easiest way to create hypnotic writing on your web site so you get the results you want is to pay attention to three essential points:

1. Use the basic three-P strategy: promise, proof, and price. If you cover those elements in your site, you will get results. Your web site will stand out above the millions that are boring.
2. Tell stories. Write about a satisfied customer. Give testimonials that have a before-and-after experience in them. Remember, stories sell and stories are how we think.
3. Write as actively as you can, using short sentences, active words, and always speaking to your reader's interests, not your own. My basic rule of thumb is to *get out of your ego* and into your visitor's ego.

Now go forth and hypnotize your visitors. Help them and they'll help you. In short, hypnotize and grow rich!

Resource Page

Summary of topics discussed in this chapter:
- ☞ What is hypnotic writing?
- ☞ The formula for causing action.
- ☞ The updated formula.
- ☞ What about your web site?
- ☞ How long is too long?
- ☞ How people think.
- ☞ How to create hypnotic stories.
- ☞ Reminders as triggers.
- ☞ Buying trances.
- ☞ Changing average writing into hypnotic writing.
- ☞ Hypnotic headline words.
- ☞ Hypnotic openings.
- ☞ Psychological copy connectors.
- ☞ Using the tips.
- ☞ Hypnotic quiz.
- ☞ Final thoughts.

Go to www.YourInternetCashMachine.com and find more hypnotic tips from Joe, as well as interviews with our guest experts. Claim your free membership now!

PART THREE

Grow Your Business!

Now you've done your preparation, mental and physical. You've chosen your business model and put your action steps into operation. Where do you go from here?

It's exciting when you first begin to make money. Heck, it's still exciting for us, even after all these years. There's no feeling like opening up e-mail in the morning and seeing a long list of paid orders pop into view!

Many Internet marketing businesses have begun in a somewhat opportunistic way—maybe yours did, too. You saw a chance to make money, and you pursued it. Definitely nothing wrong with that. But we hope by now it has begun to dawn on you that here you have potential for a serious, long-term business that can grow and support you and your family for the rest of your lives. It can send your kids to college, or even your grandkids. It can build real wealth and provide for your retirement. So let's talk about ways to grow your business.

IT'S ALL ABOUT QUALITY

We both live near Austin, Texas, which now has a greater metropolitan population of over a million people, and growing fast. When Jillian went to college here in the 1960s, Austin had 175,000 people. There were the lakes and creeks and a lot of natural beauty, a world-class university, 10 or 12 bars where you could go listen to Willie Nelson or Janis Joplin, and some excellent Mexican restaurants. That was it. A great quality of life, but still pretty much a small town. Everywhere you went, you'd see people you knew.

Today Austin is a big city. There are software companies and theatre companies, opera and ballet companies. There are freeways and very soon there will be light rail. New neighborhoods and upscale shopping centers cover the hills where cattle used to graze. Yet, in some fundamental way, Austin is still a small town. We still seldom go into a restaurant, go listen to music, or attend a sporting event where we don't see someone we know.

The Internet is like that. Hundreds of millions of people are connected through the World Wide Web, and millions of businesses are already in existence with millions more on the way. Yet, in some fascinating and mysterious way, the Internet remains a community, and within this larger community are hundreds of thousands of subsets of smaller communities, created through mutual interests.

NO PLACE TO HIDE

As an Internet business owner, you are an important and visible part of that community. The more business you do, the more visible you become. If you sell cameras to English-speaking customers, you are visible in several subset communities: buyers of electronics, camera buffs, and photographers. If you provide high-quality products and services, people will talk about you. They'll tell their friends and family, of course, but eventually they'll begin to talk about you in forums and recommend you. The people who read the forums will come and browse your site and eventually buy. Conversely, if you disappoint your customers, that word will get around, as well. There is no place to hide on the Internet.

Providing your customers with a quality experience is one of the keys to building your business. You are familiar with your product line, and you can make the best decisions as to which products to offer your customers. Your web site is easy to navigate and provides a pleasant shopping experience. By selecting a secure and reliable sales processing system, you provide an easy and safe buying experience. The remaining aspect is customer service.

DELIVER ON CUSTOMER SERVICE

One of the most frustrating experiences for any customer of an Internet business—and we know firsthand, because we both do a lot of our buying on the Internet—is not being able to communicate directly with someone in authority when there is a question or a problem. Be sure you have contact information on your web site, and be sure someone is available to answer questions or solve problems within a very short period of time. It is amazing how many web sites display an e-mail address for sending questions, but the e-mails are never answered. If you list a telephone number, be sure you or someone you designate takes the messages regularly and promptly returns calls.

As your business grows, be sure your customer service capability grows, too. When it becomes necessary, hire someone to stay in touch with your customers. At some point, you may want to contract with a service to provide live chat and full-time telephone support.

State your refund policies clearly, and honor them promptly. We recommend you set up an account for refunds, and hold a portion of your sales revenue there so you can make refunds as necessary. Most Internet marketers report requests for refunds between 2 and 10 percent, so factor that into your planning.

GO BEYOND YOUR CUSTOMER'S EXPECTATIONS

Metaphorically speaking, in your Internet business you are on one side of the counter, and your visitor, reader, or customer is on the other side. At least once a month, set aside a couple of hours and jump that counter. Put yourself in your reader's shoes. What do you want? When you interface with this (your) business, are your needs and desires being met?

What could you do for that visitor, reader, or customer to provide him with an even more satisfying experience?

From time to time, give freebies to your list. Your freebies can be in the form of reports or e-books, free teleconferences, or audio and video clips. Share interesting news with your readers. Give them tips to improve their lives and businesses.

At times it is frustrating to deal with individual customers, and there have been a few times we have unilaterally removed readers from our lists. But in general, we encourage you to love your customers. Love your visitors and the people on your list; many of them will become your customers. They enrich your life and make your lifestyle possible. Be on the lookout for ways you can enrich their lives, too. Provide as much value to them as you possibly can, not just to keep them around, but because you genuinely care for them. Spend some time every day thinking of them, sending them positive energy, and wishing them well. You'll be amazed at the results in your own world.

Our next guest expert is Bill Harris. Bill has enriched our lives, and the lives of many other people, through his Holosync technology. In the process, he's built a rock-solid Internet business and become a millionaire.

GUEST EXPERT ARTICLE

MAKE SURE YOUR CUSTOMERS ACTUALLY GET THE BENEFITS

Bill Harris

Okay, fasten your seat belt. I want to teach you something that, as far as I know, *no* other marketing guru teaches, despite the fact that it can, quite literally, double your sales—or more. I'd say that this one thing alone contributed *at least* $6 million in sales to my company in 2006. This is so simple and so obvious, you'll kick yourself when I tell you what it is.

Here it is: Make *sure* that your customers get the benefits you promised them.

That's it. Figure out what you need to do to make sure your customers get all the benefits that caused them to buy from you in the first place.

This is assuming, of course, that your product or service really does deliver benefits. If it doesn't, you need a different product. Don't laugh—this is probably the biggest reason people struggle to make money in a business: their product has limited value to others.

Think about it. If your customers really do get all the benefits your product offers, will they buy more products from you? You bet they will. They'll buy *everything you offer them*. If they really get the benefits, will they tell other people? No doubt about it. They will enthusiastically tell everyone. If your grass seed saved their lawn, they'll tell all their neighbors. If your e-book changed their life, they'll tell everyone.

These days when someone buys something and actually gets what was promised, they are so surprised, and so pleased, they can't wait to tell people. If the subject of whatever your product does comes up in conversation, they will tell others about you with evangelistic fervor.

So what do I mean when I say "make sure the customer gets all the benefits"? And how would you do that? Aren't you already putting the product in the customer's hands? Aren't you making sure he gets all the stuff you listed in your offer?

Sure. But I'm talking about making sure the customer gets all the *benefits*, which is something else altogether. So what does that mean, and how do you do it?

First, as I said, your product has to actually have benefits. If people are buying it because it *looks* like it has benefits, but it doesn't, or the benefits are trivial, or they're buying because you convinced them it has benefits when it doesn't, get another product. You can't build much of a business around a half-assed product.

Assuming your product really is good, what's the main reason why a customer would fail to benefit?

That's right! If they never use it, they'll never benefit! So, your first job is to make *sure* they use it. This could mean doing something to get them excited about trying it for the first time, before they even get it. Maybe you could send them a letter (I'd use surface mail rather than e-mail, because it will have more impact and they will be more likely to read it) reselling them on the benefits and actually *telling* them to immediately take it out of the box and use it! Trust me, if you specifically tell them to do this, more people will. If they do, they'll be more likely to get the benefits.

You could even call them a few days later, or write again, just to check in and see how they're doing, and to answer any questions they have about getting started. If you do this by letter, include a phone number they can call to ask questions.

Send something in the mail, or post it online and put the URL in the letter, giving "helpful hints on how to get the most from your new widget." Always work the benefits into anything you send, because that's what they want, and that's why they'll actually go to the trouble of using the product.

You could send something to them every couple of weeks for the first six months, reminding them of the benefits and encouraging them to actually use the product.

Now you may think I'm nuts, but did you know that most people who buy something either never use it, or use it a few times and then forget about it? Few people open the books they buy, and of those that do, few read past the first few chapters.

(Continued)

People who buy exercise equipment rarely use it after the first couple of weeks. Most people never finish self-help programs they start. And so on. I'm sure you know what I mean.

If your product is a service, you might have to point out the benefits to the customer. If you paint houses, take the customer around and point out the care you took on the windowsills, the special little detail work you did, the special way you made sure not to get paint on the window, and so on. You might also check back every six months to see how the paint job is holding up, or call and say you'd like to stop by and make sure it's holding up.

Do you see how different this is from what most people expect? Do you see, if you do these sorts of things, how good you'll look? I thought you would!

Now, what's another reason why people might not get the benefits of your product?

Yes, right again! Because they *quit* using it! Good for you. You're starting to think like a marketer.

So why would they quit? It would be different for different products, but couldn't you find out by *asking* your customers? "Are you still using your widget? No? Well tell me, why did you stop?" Find out. Then figure out how to solve the problem, whatever it is.

Maybe they quit because they ran out of a key part, or something broke. If you contacted them right about the time when you knew this might happen, and then made it super-easy to get the replacement part to them, or made it easy to get the repair done, you've solved the problem and they keep using the product. Or include the spare with the product, with a tech support number they can call to have someone walk them through how to install it. Or do whatever else might fit for your particular product.

If you think it through, you'll figure out why your customers might quit using the product. Then figure out a way to solve the problem.

Centerpointe's main product is Holosync, an audio technology which, when listened to over stereo headphones, places the listener instantly in states of super-deep meditation, delivering all the mental, emotional, and spiritual benefits of meditation in a hugely accelerated manner (www.centerpointe.com). One reason people sometimes quit using Holosync is because as they use it, unresolved emotional material can surface for some people.

So I make sure they know this might happen, why it's happening (it's actually a very beneficial thing), and what to do about it. I show them the benefit of going through this process. I also show them how to minimize any discomfort.

I do this through a series of follow-up support letters, which they receive every two weeks for the first six months. I also send them a free copy of my book, *Thresholds of the Mind*, and a multi-CD set of my talks at a Centerpointe retreat. Both have information that motivates them to continue to use the product. And I have a staff of people who do nothing all day but talk to customers and help them understand whatever is happening.

In other words, I *educate* them and hold their hand in order to make sure they keep going!

Another reason they might quit is because of the time it takes to use the product. It takes time to read a book or go through a home-study course, and some people might buy yours but never carve out the time. Figure out how to solve this problem, and more people will actually use (and benefit from) your product.

If it seems like someone might be thinking of quitting Holosync for lack of time, we have several solutions, and of course we continue to remind them of the benefits they will receive by continuing, and how much more valuable those benefits are than the little bit of time it takes to use the program.

It's also possible that a customer might quit using your product because of how they feel after using it, or while they're using it, or because there is some other side effect of using it. Figure out what these side effects might be, and figure out a solution.

Another reason people might not benefit from your product is that they don't use it correctly, or somehow sabotage themselves from getting the benefits. So figure out how a customer might do this, and then figure out how to keep it from happening. If there is a way that customers can screw things up, some of them will think of it.

Make the instructions *super* clear. Assume that the customer will figure out how to get confused, or use the product incorrectly, or possibly not notice the benefits even if they are receiving them—and

(Continued)

do whatever you can to minimize that confusion, the incorrect use of the product, or the failure to notice the benefits. Have someone standing by from whom they can get help by phone. Remind them that that person exists, and do it often.

A confession: When Centerpointe was just beginning, and I added the support letters and the telephone hotline, and the other things I do to make sure people get the benefits, everyone told me I was crazy, that all the letters would cost too much, and that talking to customers by phone would be way too time consuming.

I didn't care, though, because I was so enthusiastic about Holosync and what it does that I passionately wanted everyone to get the benefits. I wish I could say that I did all of this for business reasons, but I didn't. Only later did I discover what a brilliant *business* idea it was.

How did I discover that it was a brilliant business idea? Well, at a certain point I noticed that *half my sales* were from referrals—and I wasn't even asking for referrals (though I do now, and so should you). When I told other business owners what percentage of my customers bought more stuff from me on the back end, they were blown away! (I didn't know what percentage was normal, so I just thought everyone had so many back-end sales.)

Believe me, doing what I'm suggesting here is *so* worth doing, and hardly anyone does it. It will make you a ton of money, I promise.

Thinking this way about your business and your customers is a great example of what my marketing partner Brad Antin and I mean by "thinking like a marketer." Do you see how this isn't just a technique? It's long-range job security. And it will give you a totally unfair advantage over your competitors.

A lot of people don't see it this way (unfortunately), but your job as an entrepreneur is to provide benefits to your customers. The marketing part of your job is to show them what those benefits are, convince them that you really can deliver them, and prove that they are worth as much or more than the price they'll have to pay to get them. But can you see how easy this becomes when you do everything possible to make sure they really *get* the benefits?

When your customer tells someone else about the benefits he got, it's way more credible than when *you* tell them. And when you tell the customer about another product you have, and you really delivered on the first product, that next sale becomes a slam dunk.

So please, sit down and think this through for your business. Figure out how to get more of your customers using your product. Figure out how to keep them using it. Figure out how to keep them from sabotaging themselves and not getting the benefits. Figure out how to keep them from failing to notice the benefits when they get them.

If you do this, you're beginning to think like a marketer, and your business—and your profits—will expand.

Bill Harris co-developed the Holosync Solution program, which utilizes Centerpointe's proprietary Holosync sound technology, embedded beneath soothing music and environmental sounds, to induce deep meditative states, causing the brain to reorganize at higher levels of functioning. Bill currently serves as president and director of Centerpointe Research Institute (www.Centerpointe.com).

Resource Page

Summary of topics discussed in this chapter:
- ☞ No place to hide.
- ☞ Deliver on customer service.
- ☞ Go beyond your customer's expectations.

Guest expert Bill Harris offers an article on making sure your customers get the benefits.

Go to www.YourInternetCashMachine.com and to take advantage of much more information about your Internet business, as well as interviews with our guest experts. Claim your free membership now!

BUILD YOUR BUSINESS SUPPORT NETWORK

O perating an Internet business can be deeply satisfying for those of us who are entrepreneurs. If you cherish your time alone, you will find that an Internet business provides some great secondary benefits. However, it can be lonely. There is also a drawback from a practical business perspective, because there is often no one else with whom you can bounce around your ideas and discuss potential solutions to your problems. Your spouse may want to be supportive, but unless he or she works in the same or a similar business, much of what you're talking about will sound like Greek.

THE POWER OF THE MASTERMIND GROUP

We are fortunate to have friends with Internet businesses, and we talk with them by phone and e-mail. But our greatest support has come through our mastermind groups. For a number of years we were in a weekly mastermind group together, and Joe is in another group now. Joe and our friend Bill Hibbler wrote a very popular book on masterminding last year, to which Jillian contributed. The book is *Meet and Grow Rich* (John Wiley & Sons, 2006), and we encourage you to buy a copy. It's available through Amazon and other bookstores. We've asked Bill to act as our guest expert on mastermind groups.

GUEST EXPERT ARTICLE

MASTERMIND GROUPS FOR INTERNET MARKETERS

Bill Hibbler

Succeeding in your online business isn't easy. It's easy to feel overwhelmed and alone. Imagine, then, if you had a support group to advise, encourage, and help you focus on your goals. What if this group became a powerful alliance to create joint ventures, share resources, and build your business faster? Would you like to have such a group?

Groups like this are being formed all across the globe. They're called *mastermind* groups. Mastermind groups bring together individuals like you who seek to achieve their personal and collective goals, whether for wealth, health, or something else. Internet marketing is the primary theme of my current mastermind group, Siglo IV.

A mastermind group can be beneficial for anyone, but there are additional benefits for those who make their living online. Internet marketers usually work out of a home office, which means we tend to be isolated. Our customers and peers are all over the world but we rarely meet them in person. Usually the only time we have any face-to-face contact is at live seminars. So, in addition to all the other benefits, the group meetings are also a social setting for us. But there are many benefits to an Internet marketing mastermind.

In our group, members have created products together, spoken at each other's live seminars and teleseminars, and promoted each other's products to our mailing lists. Besides doing joint ventures, there are a number of resources that can be shared, such as:

- ☞ Web site designers.
- ☞ Graphic designers.

(Continued)

- ☞   Web site automation services.
- ☞   Virtual assistants.
- ☞   Product fulfillment companies.
- ☞   Print-on-demand publishers.
- ☞   Teleseminar and web conferencing services.
- ☞   Online audio and video software and services.
- ☞   Programmers.
- ☞   Autoresponder services.
- ☞   Co-registration services.

And the list goes on and on. Rather than using cheap shared hosting, members can go in on a dedicated server for their web sites. So rather than paying $20 a month to a company where your web site shares a server with hundreds or even thousands of other sites, for about the same money, five or six of you can share a fast, state of the art web server, which means your web sites will load faster for visitors and are far less likely to have downtime. You can also compare notes on joint venture partners, affiliate software, e-book software, Internet marketing courses, other software, and so on.

So how many members do you need in your mastermind group? For most types of groups, ideally, you want five to six members. When you have more, meetings can drag on too long. If each member gets 20 minutes and you've got six members, that's two hours. Getting the meeting started, taking a short break in the middle, and wrapping things up will add a half hour. That's two and a half hours. Beyond that is too long, especially if you meet once a week. So if you choose to go with more than six members, we'd recommend limiting each person's turn to 10 or 15 minutes.

However, when you have fewer than five members, meetings are unproductive when one or two people can't make it. You'll end up either canceling meetings or having people drop out.

How often should your group meet? I've had groups that met weekly and groups that met every other week. My preference is meeting either weekly or monthly. Many prefer weekly meetings because they like the consistent rhythm. If you meet every other week, you spend too much time recounting what you've been up to since the last meeting. Plus if you miss a meeting, you're out of the loop for a month.

However, I've had groups that met monthly and have been quite successful. Also, you might try meeting once a week for a while and then cutting back if the group feels that schedule is too restrictive.

Where should you meet? A mastermind group requires a quiet, private place where people feel comfortable sitting for two to three hours. Select a spot with space to park that's safe and convenient for everyone in the group. That might be a conference room in an office building, or a private room in a library, church, community center, or restaurant. Some mastermind groups choose to meet in members' homes. Either they meet at the same place every week or rotate with a different member playing host each week. If you decide on the latter approach, make sure every member of the group is comfortable with the idea.

How do you find people to mastermind with? I believe rather than trying to find four or five mastermind partners at once, it's better to start out seeking a single person. Find one person with similar goals with whom you resonate. Meet once or twice (or more) and start to build a relationship and be sure you get along well. Then, together, seek a third mastermind partner.

When you find that potential partner, invite him to join on a trial basis. If things go well with the new member, invite him to become a permanent member of the group. If you don't feel comfortable with the new member by the end of the trial period, thank him for his time and start looking for a new third partner.

Once you have your permanent third member, the three of you can seek out a fourth member. You'll continue this process until you've got a solid group of five or six members.

Mastermind groups have proven themselves effective for everything from emotional support to financial support. Some of the greatest tycoons in history have used mastermind groups, from Andrew Carnegie to Dale Carnegie. They can work for you, too.

(Continued)

Bill Hibbler is the co-author (with Joe Vitale) of Meet and Grow Rich. *For more information about how to form your own mastermind group, visit www .MeetandGrowRich.com. For Internet marketing tips, tricks and product and service reviews, sign up for Bill's free newsletter, "Ecommerce Confidential" at www.Ecommerce Confidential.com.*

THE FINE ART OF DELEGATION

One of the most vital lessons you can learn as an entrepreneur, and particularly as an Internet marketer, is to delegate. Every person has a few *core competencies*. Identify yours, and focus your efforts in those areas. Let the rest go.

For example, Jillian is a conceptual thinker who can generate product ideas. She is a good writer and marketer. She is a big-picture person. She is not technically adept, nor does she have good clerical and organizational skills. Dempsey, her husband, is a natural when it comes to the technical side. So he manages the sites and creates all the behind-the-scenes magic. (He also operates a music site, www.DempseysMusic .com, and a number of affiliate sites.) Matt, her son, is a film student. He handles the video—at least until he becomes rich and famous in his own right—as well as his film site, www.MattColemanFilms.com. Nieces Brittany and Kaleem contribute clerical skills around their college work. Over the years Jillian has also assembled a great team of contractors: grant consultants, virtual assistants, graphic artists, copywriters, and a Director of Marketing who handles her affiliate program and joint ventures.

Joe is a concept person, a marketer, and a very prolific writer. His team includes Suzanne, the best public relations and personal assistant anyone could ever have; a webmaster; virtual assistants; graphic artists; copywriters; and his personally trained team of Hypnotic Marketing and Miracles coaches. He also has a relationship with a separate company that distributes many of his products and manages affiliate relationships. Of course, we both have a number of joint venture partnerships.

The point here is, don't try to do everything. Do the things *only you* can do. Any work that can be competently performed by someone else, delegate. A good rule of thumb is to think about which activities bring in money. If you are doing something that takes up your time and doesn't directly generate money, find someone else to do it. If you can choose between two different activities, do the one that generates the most money.

Either of us could spend time on the phone setting up new joint ventures. We're both good at selling ourselves and our projects. However, that would not be the best use of our time. We have other people who are good at that. What no one else can do is access the ideas in our heads and write them down. No one else can generate the product ideas we think of, although other people can help us create them.

Sometimes the other people in our businesses also have great project ideas, and we joint-venture with them. We are creative people, and we love to foster creativity. We have learned this primary equation: $C + E + CC = \$$, meaning creativity plus efficiency plus customer care equals money.

The other members of our teams are the business experts. We recommend you find a good attorney and a good accountant. Spend time doing research and get the best tax and legal advice available. The next two chapters of this book address those issues.

Resource Page

Summary of topics discussed in this chapter:
☞ The power of the mastermind group.
☞ The fine art of delegation.

Guest expert Bill Hibbler writes about how to set up a mastermind group to support your Internet business.

Go to www.YourInternetCashMachine.com and access a variety of resources, as well as interviews with our guest experts. Claim your free membership now!

COMPLY WITH CYBER LAW

T he trade-off for living in a civil society is the necessity of
following a body of laws. While Internet business owners
face fewer restrictions than many other businesses, there are
laws that apply to us. The two of us are not attorneys, of
course, and we are not giving you legal advice. However, based on our
research, here is some basic information you need to know.

SPAM

Spam is the commonly accepted term for unsolicited e-mail messages,
and the proliferation of spam on the Internet has caused problems for
all Internet marketers. The e-mails we send have to compete with the
hundreds of millions of spam e-mails sent every day. Our readers may
fail to recognize our e-mails, or be so irritated by the onslaught of ads
for pornography and drugs that they immediately delete our messages
along with the spam. Worse still, they may mark our e-mails as spam,
causing their Internet service provider to block our e-mails until we
can prove the reader subscribed to our list.

The CAN-SPAM Act of 2003 is the U.S. government's response to
spam (CAN-SPAM is an acronym for the full name of the bill, Control-
ling the Assault of Non-Solicited Pornography and Marketing Act of 2003).
This act covers all Internet businesses, but exempts personal e-mail. Under
the law, Internet business owners must ensure that every e-mail message
we send out includes the following four elements:

1. An opt-out link, so the reader may unsubscribe.
2. A valid subject line and accurate routing information.
3. The correct e-mail address of the sender.
4. A label if the e-mail contains adult content.

Of course, the hardcore spammers completely ignore the law. Only a few people have been prosecuted under the act, which has proven hugely ineffective in actually stopping spam. Nevertheless, legitimate Internet marketers must exercise great care. If you are using a professional autoresponder service (such as www.CashMachineCart .com), you can rest assured your e-mails will be properly structured and the law carefully observed.

COPYRIGHTS

There is easy access to so much information on the Internet, both written and graphic material, it can be tempting to borrow. However, the Copyright Act applies on the Internet as in other forms of publishing. Using third-party text without permission or direct citation opens you up to legal liability. Make sure your content is original. The same principle applies to photographs and drawings. Once a string of text or an image is fixed for the first time on a hard drive, copyright is established.

You can purchase software with free photographs and images. There are also web sites that provide graphic images for reuse under licensing, although many of them are expensive. Visit www.YourInternet CashMachine.com for our recommendations.

TRADEMARKS

Using trademarks to identify products on your web site is not illegal, but in some cases trademark owners have attempted to aggressively protect their trademarks by claiming violations. Your responsibility is to avoid violating existing trademarks by creating new marks that are too similar or confusing to readers, which may cause trademark infringement.

In creating your own trademark, it is best to create a new word, or use an existing word in a truly distinctive manner. Then perform a trademark search through the U.S. Patent and Trademark Office, to be sure your mark is not already taken. We suggest you then proceed with a federal trademark registration. Although there are companies, and attorneys, who will do this for you, the process is quite simple, if time consuming.

FREE SPEECH

The Internet has created an amazing community in which people feel empowered to speak freely and openly. In your Internet business, you will enjoy some of that freedom. However, you are still subject to some legal restrictions. In particular, it is wise to exercise care you do not defame another person or organization. *Defamation* is an untrue statement which is damaging to a person or organization's reputation, and the law surrounding it is complex. The bottom line is, you never want to have to spend money defending yourself against a defamation lawsuit, so think before you write.

Our next guest expert, Bob Silber, is an attorney. He advises many of the top Internet marketers, and we have asked him to identify the legal issues he considers critical for Internet business owners.

GUEST EXPERT ARTICLE

LEGAL ISSUES FOR INTERNET MARKETERS

Bob Silber

A recurring question from Internet marketers is "What is the biggest legal mistake people make with their online business?"

Representing Internet marketers who are just starting out building their businesses, as well as marketers who make millions of dollars a year, I find the answer remains the same. You should treat your online business as a real business. That, of course, can cover a broad range of good business practices.

For example, a businessperson who wouldn't think of operating a bricks-and-mortar business without legally protecting himself with a limited liability entity, such as a corporation or limited liability company, often operates an online business without such protection. It shouldn't come as news that we live in a litigious society, and

---

without such protection, your business and personal assets are at risk. If you fall into this category, you should consult with your accountant, determine what limited liability entity is right for you, and take advantage of this legal protection.

Although many agencies are involved in policing the Internet, the Federal Trade Commission (FTC) is the main regulatory agency in the United States and pursues vigorous and effective law enforcement against business violators both online and off. The FTC regulates advertising and business practices with strict rules, regulations, and laws to protect both businesses and consumers. All advertising media, including direct mail, print media, television, radio, and the Internet are subject to the FTC rules and regulations.

Every businessperson should visit the FTC web site at FTC.gov and familiarize themselves with the various rules and regulations for doing business on the Internet. Spending some time at the FTC web site is a good way to educate yourself about the rules of the road for Internet businesses.

Another area for legal concern is your web site sales copy. Your web site sales copy should be truthful and free of hyperbole. Hiring an established copywriter is a wise investment as it is a delicate balancing act to write effective sales copy that converts to sales and also complies with the FTC rules and regulations.

You must have the proper legal documents, such as a privacy policy, on your web site. In addition to a web site privacy policy, you should consider a terms of service agreement, commonly referred to as a TOS. Other common legal documents are legal disclaimers and warranties. Consulting with your lawyer to determine what legal documents you should have on your web site to be legally compliant is good business and can prevent legal problems down the road.

Choosing and registering the proper domain name is important for your business. Once you have decided on your domain name, you should visit the U.S. Patent and Trademark Office Web site at USPTO.gov and do a preliminary search to see if anyone has trademarked the same or a similar name. If you find that the same or a similar name has been trademarked, then you need to go back to the drawing board, choose another name, and repeat the search. It is disheartening to have put time, money, and effort into building a

(Continued)

business brand around your business name, only to receive a cease-and-desist letter for violating someone's trademark.

You must be careful of infringing on another's trademark, whether by registering domain names with misspellings of a trademark or domain names that can be considered similar to a trademark.

Remember to treat your Internet business as a real business, and you can make money while avoiding the common problems that others encounter.

Bob Silber is one of the world's most respected authorities on Internet marketing law. He is an attorney, consultant, speaker, author, and former adjunct professor teaching business, e-commerce, intellectual property, and Internet law at a major university. His clients include best-selling authors, high-paid speakers, the Internet's most successful marketers, and up-and-coming business owners.

Bob is legal counsel to the Internet superstars. His Internet marketing clients read like a who's who of Internet marketing, and include individuals generating millions of dollars annually on the Web. You can subscribe to his popular free newsletter for Internet marketers at BobSilberLetter.com.

Resource Page

Summary of topics discussed in this chapter:
- ☛ Understand and avoid spam.
- ☛ Comply with copyright law.
- ☛ Observe trademark law.
- ☛ Rights and responsibilities of free speech.

Guest expert attorney Bob Silber writes about cyber law considerations for Internet marketers.

Go to www.YourInternetCashMachine.com and find more resources on Internet law, as well as interviews with our guest experts. Claim your free membership now!

PLAN FOR SUCCESS

An Internet business presents you with a unique opportunity to go into business for yourself with a minimal initial investment, no employees, and little infrastructure. Still, there are practical decisions to be made in any business, and here we present a few guidelines for your consideration.

YOUR BUSINESS PLAN

Our guess is that some readers will see this heading and their eyes will immediately glaze over. Others will get excited and begin mentally rubbing their hands together in anticipation. If you are a born organizer, writing a business plan will seem easy. If not, we encourage you to keep an open mind as we walk you through the process.

Let's begin with *why*. Why write a business plan? Why not just jump in and get started? Well, that's exactly what many entrepreneurs do. First they establish the business; then, when they begin to see the value, they work on their business plan. We're not arguing for a hard-and-fast approach, but we do recommend that at some point, fairly early in the process of getting your business off the ground, you give yourself the gift of completing a business plan.

A business plan is useful if you ever want to borrow money, or if you decide to seek investment capital. However, the main benefit of a business plan is that it helps you assess your overall business situation, make strategic decisions, and plan the tactical steps that will enable your business to be profitable and grow.

A business plan is not a static document. You don't write it, put it in a drawer, and forget about it. A business plan is an outline of your best thinking at any given time. For a business plan to truly serve you, you write it, then review it at least quarterly for as long as you own your business. Thus your revised business plan reflects all you learn as you operate your business, and all the decisions you make as a result.

Formats for business plans vary. Here is a basic outline of the four essential elements:

1. *Executive summary*. This is a page or two that summarizes the high points of all the other sections.
2. *Organization*. Here you will write your mission statement, one sentence that describes the purpose of your business. Outline your business philosophy and your goals. Briefly detail the history of the business and its legal status (individual owner, partnership, corporation). Describe the management team, which may be only you, or may include employees and/or contractors.
3. *Marketing plan*. In this section, describe your marketplace niche and your potential customers, competition, products, pricing structure, and delivery systems. Outline your marketing strategy, based on the promotional methods we described in the chapter, "Get the Word Out."
4. *Operational plan*. Here you describe the day-to-day operation of your business and your plans for expansion. This may include your anticipated investment in new software, hardware, education, and staffing. Your finances will be part of this section. What are the anticipated start-up costs for your business, if you have not already expensed them? How will you raise any needed capital?

   If you have borrowed money for your business, what is your repayment plan? How much money do you need every month, both personally and for your business? What are your fixed and recurrent expenses? How will you meet those expenses as you build your business? Complete your financial forecast for the next six months and for the next year.

Allow plenty of time to write your business plan. It is not something you can do in one sitting. If you are married, involve your spouse. This is a plan that affects your personal as well as professional life. If you work with a mastermind group or have friends whose advice you value, ask for their input. You can begin writing in any section, but leave the executive summary for last.

Jillian has developed software specifically for the Internet business plan. You can access it on our web site, www.YourInternetCashMachine .com (see the Resource page).

INCORPORATION

As we said earlier, we are not attorneys, and we cannot give you legal advice. The following comments express our best understanding of the issues, and you should seek the advice of your own professional legal counsel before taking any action. That said, we believe incorporation will provide you with a number of benefits.

The first benefit is protection. If you set your business up as a corporation, it will be recognized as a legal entity unto itself. You must take care to keep your business completely separate from your personal business life, so as not to pierce the corporate veil. If you do that, should you ever be sued, the lawsuit would affect only the corporation, and not you personally. All of your personal assets would be safe and protected. Many business owners establish several corporations to create a legal wall between their different business activities and assets.

Corporations also enjoy some benefits not available to individual business owners. For example, some health, life, and long-term care insurance is available to corporations only. Insurance benefits can be provided from before-tax income. A corporation can also provide other benefits to its employees, such as educational benefits. In practical terms, that means if you employ your college-age children, you can pay their college tuition in before-tax dollars.

There are several types of corporations. C corporations and S corporations are the traditional ones, and limited liability corporations (LLC) are becoming increasingly popular. Some states, such as Delaware and Nevada, are considered to have particularly business-friendly corporate laws. A lot of information is available on the Internet, so do your research and understand the issues before you make a final decision. When dealing with an attorney, we recommend you select someone who specializes in business law and who has clients with Internet businesses.

In planning for the future, knowledge is power. Our final guest expert is Mike Mograbi, the best-selling author of 378 *Internet Marketing Predictions*. Mike lives and works in Lebanon, and we asked him to prognosticate from a global perspective.

GUEST EXPERT ARTICLE

HOW TO PREDICT YOUR WAY TO WEALTH

Mike Mograbi

Consider the following predictions, made by experts:

- ☞ "This 'telephone' has too many shortcomings to be seriously considered as a means of communication. The device is inherently of no value to us." (Western Union internal memo, 1876)
- ☞ "We don't like their sound, and guitar music is on the way out." (Decca Recording Company rejecting the Beatles in 1962)
- ☞ "The phonograph . . . is not of any commercial value." (Thomas Edison remarking on his own invention to his assistant, Sam Insull, 1880)
- ☞ "Sensible and responsible women do not want to vote." (Grover Cleveland, 1905)
- ☞ "It is an idle dream to imagine that . . . automobiles will take the place of railways in the long-distance movement of . . . passengers." (American Road Congress, 1913)
- ☞ "There is no likelihood man can ever tap the power of the atom." (Robert Millikan, Nobel Prize winner in physics, 1920.)
- ☞ "The odds are now that the United States will not be able to honor the 1970 manned-lunar-landing date set by Mr. Kennedy." (*New Scientist*, April 30, 1964)
- ☞ "The bomb will never go off. I speak as an expert in explosives." (Admiral William Leahy, U.S. Atomic Bomb Project, 1943)
- ☞ "The wireless music box has no imaginable commercial value. Who would pay for a message sent to nobody in particular?" (David Sarnoff's associates in response to his urgings for investment in the radio in the 1920s)

☞ "There is no reason anyone would want a computer in their home." (Ken Olsen, president of Digital Equipment Corporation, 1977)

☞ "Who the hell wants to hear actors talk?" (Harry Warner, Warner Brothers Pictures, 1927)

☞ "I think there is a world market for about five computers." (Thomas Watson, chairman of IBM, 1943)

☞ "Flight by machines heavier than air is unpractical and insignificant, if not utterly impossible." (Simon Newcomb, an astronomer of some note, 1902)

☞ "Man will never reach the moon regardless of all future scientific advances." (Dr. Lee DeForest, inventor, 1957)

☞ "Heavier-than-air flying machines are impossible." (Lord Kelvin, president, Royal Society, 1895)

☞ "640K ought to be enough for anybody." (Bill Gates, 1981)

Source: Paradigms—The Business of Discovering the Future by Joel Arthur Barker (Collins, 1993), an excellent book on the subject of the business of discovering the future.

What would make experts and people with great minds like the ones just quoted make such humorous predictions? The answer can be found in one word: the blinding power of *paradigms*.

Break Out of Your Paradigms

Even experts and professionals are sometimes unable to look past their own paradigms. What exactly is a paradigm? It's a set of beliefs, rules, and regulations (written or unwritten) that does two things: (1) it establishes or defines boundaries (mental, behavioral, etc.), and (2) it tells you how to think and behave inside the boundaries in order to be successful.

Paradigms determine how people perceive the world. People see best what they believe they are supposed to see. Prevailing paradigms determine that. Also, people see poorly, or not at all, information and data that does not fit into their paradigms. They are literally unable to see things right before their very eyes.

(Continued)

Here's what you have to know: The future of your business exists just outside the boundaries of your industry's prevailing paradigm(s). Free yourself from the mentally enslaving and paralyzing power of prevailing paradigms and you'll see how easy it becomes to come up with amazing discoveries and innovations.

A *paradigm shift* occurs when there is a breakout from an old paradigm into a new set of rules. Therefore, to be able to see the future and make accurate predictions, you must:

☞   Think twice before you say "Impossible." Remember, advances in technology are making the impossible possible. What seems impossible today is so only in the context of present paradigms.
☞   Look past the prevailing paradigm(s).
☞   Watch the rule breakers: Keep a close eye on professional people messing with the rules, because that is the earliest sign of significant change.

And when the rules change, the whole world can change.

Define an Industry or Market

Okay, so you want to make predictions about the future. The question is, the future of what? The stock market? Internet marketing? Computer games? Which market?

In order to make predictions about the future you have to define your target market. Then know your industry and your market *thoroughly*. Accurate predictions mandate that you know your target market inside-out.

Do you know what you need *to base your predictions on?* Solid facts! Without solid facts your predictions will be nothing more than baseless speculations. Here's a simple example for you to see what I mean. Your child is playing in the living room and right there on the table near her is a chocolate bar that she hasn't noticed yet. Now, you know two facts: (1) your child loves sweets, and (2) your child has not yet noticed the chocolate bar. Based on these facts, you can predict with a high level of accuracy and certainty that the millisecond she sees the chocolate bar she's going to reach out for it.

The more you study your industry or market, the more solid facts you'll have upon which to base your predictions. Start learning and devouring everything related to your industry/market. Know your industry, and your market, inside-out. The more you study, the more solid facts you'll have upon which to base your predictions.

Go to online bookstores like Amazon.com and comb the resources related to your business, industry, and target market. Subscribe to all online and off-line newsletters and publications related to your industry and market. Comb the Internet, bookmark all the sites related to your industry/market, and make sure you check them periodically. Use the Web information company Alexa (www.alexa .com) to check important web site rankings and to identify related web sites.

Don't worry about not being omniscient in your field. By doing what I'm telling you, you will find your intuitive judgment and human creativity will skyrocket and you'll soon be able to make increasingly accurate predictions even with incomplete data.

Know Where the Future is Coming From

It's coming from the present! What's going to happen to you and your business in the near future is determined by what you're doing and manufacturing today. The future has its roots in today. If you plant an apple seed today, you'll have an apple tree tomorrow. Well, maybe not tomorrow, but the point is you won't get a peach tree, that's for sure!

If you eat salty food now you're going to be thirsty and you're going to need water in the near future. Most people cannot and do not perceive all the consequences of what they're doing today. Signs of the future are all around us, but it isn't until much later that most of the world realizes their significance.

In order to make accurate predictions about the future, think of the consequences of what we're doing today. Think especially in terms of what problems, difficulties, and challenges we might face in the near future as a result and consequence of what we're doing today.

(Continued)

Keep an Eye on Alpha, Beta, and Emerging Technologies

New technologies enable you to develop new solutions that were not possible in the past. They enable you to develop improved and better solutions, overcoming the limitations, weaknesses, and short-comings of today's solutions.

Know what new technology solutions are being developed for your industry or business. One of the best ways (though not the only way) is to keep a very close eye on alpha and beta news.

What is *alpha* and *beta* news? Technology applications and software solutions usually go through alpha and beta testing before being launched to the world.

By following up on alpha/beta news, you get to know what new products and solutions are going to be offered to your industry/market before they actually are. One useful site you can check out is www.BetaNews.com.

The importance of emerging technology in determining the future of almost everything on our planet is growing exponentially. Learn and be up-to-date about emerging technologies. Ask yourself how such technologies might impact your industry and how you can be the first to capitalize on it. Keep a very close eye on the techies out there who are messing around with your industry rules.

People who know their industry very well and know how to utilize the latest technologies to solve its most immediate and pressing problems (the ones that existing products are failing to solve) always make a lot of money.

New technologies set new and higher limits of what we can do. They redefine what is possible.

Identify Problems and Come Up with Innovative Solutions

This is easier than you think! Given the fact that you're now free from the shackles of prevailing paradigms, you can think more clearly and innovatively than your peers and competitors. Identify problems faced by your industry, ones that your industry really wants to solve but doesn't have the slightest idea how.

The formula is very simple, really. If you can identify problems faced by your industry, business, or market, and come up with solutions to these problems, then you will have actually invented the future.

How can you come up with innovative solutions? The magical answer is: Question the way things are currently being done. The most powerful, million-dollar question you have to keep asking is "Who said things have to be done this way?" Who says things should be done the way they're being done?

Who said watches have to have hands, springs, bearings, and so on.? You see, it was Swiss researchers who invented the electronic quartz movement at their research institute in Neuchatel, Switzerland. When this revolutionary new idea was presented to Swiss manufacturers in 1967, it was rejected. Why? Because it didn't have a mainspring, it didn't need bearings, it required almost no gears, and it was battery powered. It was electronic. It couldn't possibly be the watch of the future.

A word of advice: Don't just focus on solving the easy problems, because you can rest assured that 99.9 percent of your competitors are working on solving them. It is human nature to work on solving the easy problems first. You can get an amazingly clear idea of what's cookin' by closely following your industry news.

Instead, try to tackle the slightly harder problems. You won't find many people on that territory. The more difficult the problem, the fewer people you'll find competing against you!

Discover New Solutions for Improving the Way Your Market Is Currently Doing Things

Let's focus on solutions that improve the way your industry is currently doing things. The question you want to ask is "How can we do this thing in a better, more efficient way?"

However, the most important questions you need to ask are "What do people want? How can we give it to them more efficiently and effectively for us both?"

(Continued)

Always think of the end result and ultimate goal. Give people what they want, when they want it, how they want it, where they want it, in the easiest, fastest, and most effortless ways. Encyclopedias could be written on this statement.

Don't think of offering people what they want in terms of products, or you might get locked up with those mainsprings, bearings, gears, and hands. Fax and e-mail are communication technologies used to send and receive information. The keywords are *communication* and *information*. Do people want a fax machine or do they want a way to send and receive information quickly, easily, and effortlessly?

ICQ, the online communications company, did not create a new fax machine or an improved e-mail system. ICQ answered this question by being the first to create instant messaging in the mid-1990s. After a few years, AOL acquired ICQ for $283 million!

Got the point? Don't think products. Think solutions that would become products.

Use Divergent Thinking

One of the components of strategic exploration is *divergent thinking*. It is the thinking skill necessary for discovering more than one right answer. Generally speaking, to any given problem there is more than one possible solution. This is best explained and illustrated in an example.

Let's consider e-mail publishing of newsletters and e-zines. The problem to the subscriber is spam. The problem to the publisher is the filtering of legitimate e-mails. Here are two potential solutions: (1) spam filters, spam checkers, and changing words, or (2) the use of RSS/XML feeds, news readers, and aggregators.

Always make sure you think of the two types of possible solutions—one that is related to products currently being used and one that is *totally unrelated*. Solution 1 is an *enhancing* solution or innovation that improves upon what we already have. Solution 2 is a *shifting* innovation.

In general, people are resistant to shifting innovations because they involve learning and changing the way we currently do things.

They require us to budge from our comfort zone. However, it is such solutions, introduced at the right time, that make those seven- and eight-figure incomes!

Look at and Focus on the Near Future

The further out in time you try to look, the foggier it gets and the less accurate your predictions become. Nobody can make accurate predictions of the distant future. One of the main reasons for this is lack of information and data. Simply put, we have no clue or idea what technologies will be available in the distant future that might *totally*—not just partially—change the way we do things.

What is impossible today is only so in the context of present technologies and resources. The distant future is simply impossible to see. Focus on the near future!

Look at the Past and Learn from It

We cannot always determine what's going to happen in the future by looking at the past, but we can learn a lot from it. That's right. We learn from history that many so-called new and amazing things flop in version 1.0 in the year 7750 but succeed beyond imagination in the year 7800. Every month, many superb solutions are introduced before their prime time. The problem lies in the timing, not the solution. Therefore, be very careful of statements like, "We tried something like that before and it didn't work."

Tomorrow's Technologies and Solutions Won't Wipe Out Today's

There are two main reasons for this. First, people are slow to adopt anything new, even if it makes their lives easier. Transitions are slow. It takes quite some time for old technologies and solutions to die out. The more widely used something is, the more time it takes

(Continued)

the world to make the transition. Second, new technologies and solutions could be complementary to today's solutions.

Today, we have snail mail, fax, and e-mail; printed books and e-books; HTML and Flash web sites; and RSS publishing. In the future, we'll have both 2D and 3D web sites, and so on.

Always think *both/and* before thinking *either/or*.

Mike Mograbi is an Internet marketer and creator of many Internet marketing products and services. In mid-2004 he wrote the best-selling, highly acclaimed e-book 378 Internet Marketing Predictions. *He runs the leading Internet marketing news web site, Internet Marketing Newswatch (www.imnewswatch.com).*

Resource Page

Summary of topics discussed in this chapter:
- ☛ Write your business plan.
- ☛ Decide upon incorporation.

This chapter's guest expert, Mike Mograbi, offers his predictions on future trends in Internet business.

Go to www.YourInternetCashMachine.com and get access to our Internet business plan software, as well as interviews with our guest experts. Claim your free membership now!

INDEX

A

Action, 121, 128, 159–162
Administrative interface, web hosting and, 110
Adult sites, gambling and, 46–48
Advertising, 27, 28, 149
Affiliate, 70, 71–72
Affiliate networks, 72, 75
Affiliate program directories, 75
Affiliate programs:
  online business marketing and, 139–140
  selling informational products for, 93
  types of, 70–71
  in Web sites, 113–114
Affiliate sales sites:
  advantages of, 70–71
  building business using, 33–34
  content in, 77–78
  Google AdSense, 78–79
  making money as affiliate, 71–72
  selecting merchant partners, 72–77
American gambling businesses, 46–47
Anthony, Robert, 168–170
Armstrong, Heather, 28
Articles:
  as information products, 87–88
  Web site traffic and, 128–129
The Attractor Factor (Vitale), 36
Auction, 57–58, 60, 61
Auction sites, 33, 58–59
Audio recordings:
  as information products, 88
  Web site traffic and, 147
Autoresponders, in Web sites, 112–113

B

Bells and whistles, 64, 131
Beyond Positive Thinking (Anthony), 168
Blog(s):
  MySpace, 82
  role of, 28–31
  search engines and, 132–133
  Web sites ranking and, 130
Born, James O., 32
Branding, 134
Browser-based news readers, 31
"Build Your List with Pay Per Click" (Leung), 150–152
Burning, in software, 98
Business. *See also* Off-line business; Online business
  building support network to grow, 194–199
  complying with cyber law to grow, 200–204
  personal life and, 4–5
  planning for success to grow, 205–216
  quality and, 185–193
  treating online business as, 63
Business Opportunity Rule, 41–42
Business plan, 205–207
"Buying Trances: The Real Secret to Hypnotic Selling" (Vitale), 171–176
Buy/trade advertising, Web site traffic and, 149

C

Call to action, 121, 128
CAN-SPAM Act of 2003, 200
Career, creating abundance in, 11–15

CashMachineCart site, 114
CashMachineDomains site, 111, 117, 133
ClickBank site, 73, 76, 90, 99
Cochrum, Jim, 65–69
Companies, affiliate programs and selecting, 75
Content:
　　in affiliate sales sites, 77–78
　　joint ventures and quality of, 139
　　of Web site, 131
Conversion strategy, business success and, 143
Copy connectors, 179
Copyright, 117, 201
Corporations, types of, 207–208
Cost per action (CPA), 71
Cost per click (CPC), 72
Cost per impression (CPM), 72
Cost per sale (CPS), 72
CPA. *See* Cost per action (CPA)
CPC. *See* Cost per click (CPC)
CPM. *See* Cost per impression (CPM)
CPS. *See* Cost per sale (CPS)
"Creating Abundance in Your Career"
　　(Pauley), 11–15
Cuban, Mark, 13
Customers, 85, 187
Customer service, 110, 186–187
Cyber law, complying with, 200–204

D

Dark Blue site, 73–74
Data capture strategy, 144
Dating sites, 34–35
Delegation, fine art of, 198–199
Delivery, of information products, 89, 90, 92
Demand, 88–89, 56
Design, of Web sites, 114–117, 131
Desires, Internet business and, 8–10
Direct sales. *See* Multilevel marketing (MLM)
Domain name, 106, 107–110
Downloadable products, 89, 90
Drop shipping, 61
Dutch auction, 57–58

E

eBay:
　　auction times at, 61
　　background and benefits of, 50–51
　　buying for resale on, 58–59
　　getting started on, 51–54
　　leveraging, 64–65
　　opening store at, 25
　　powerSellers in, 62–63
　　pricing auction items, 56–58
　　search engine, 60
　　tools utilized by sellers, 64
　　using MySpace to grow, 81–82
　　what to sell on, 54–56
"eBay and Beyond" (Cochrum)
E-books selling, 67–68
"Educating for Entrepreneurship" (Perry),
　　38–40
Education sites, 37–38
Edwards, Jim, 145–147
E-mail addresses, collecting, 117
E-mail marketing, 127–128
Entertainment sites, 31–33
*Everything I Know About Business, I Learned From
　　My Mama* (Knox), 95
Exclusive and non-exclusive agreement, 76
Exit traffic, 149
Expertise, 7–8
E-Zine-mail newsletter, business success
　　and, 144

F

Facebook site, 35–36, 80
Federal Trade Commission (FTC), 41–42,
　　203
Five P's (promise, product, package, price,
　　and penalty), in writing sales letters, 122
Free speech, 202
Friesen, Wendi, 152–155
FTC. *See* Federal Trade Commission (FTC)

G

Gambling and adult sites, 46–48
General information sites, 26–28
Geometric earning, 45
"Geometric Giving: The Easy Way to Donate
　　$1 Million a Month to Charity" (Sabol),
　　43–46
"Get Your Real Estate Business Online"
　　(Goins), 21–23
Ginsberg, Adam, 81–83
Goins, Larry, 21–23
Google:
　　AdSense, 35, 78–79
　　AdWords, 150–151
　　for pricing research, 56–57
　　search engine optimization, 129–131
　　searching affiliate networks in, 75
　　Toolbar, 130
　　Video, 100
Googlebot, 130

H

Harris, Bill, 187, 188–193
Hendricks, Mark, 120, 121–126
Heyer, Sam, 83–86
Hibbler, Bill, 77, 195–197
How to Buy, Sell, and Profit on eBay (Ginsberg), 82
"How To Make and Sell a Video Product at Zero Cost" (Oden), 95–100
"How to Predict Your Way to Wealth" (Mograbi), 2–8, 216
Hypnotic writing, Web sites and, 34, 158–181
Hyponic Marketing Inc., 34

I

I'm Rich Beyond My Wildest Dreams - I am. I am. I am. (Pauley and Pauley), 13
Income, of affiliate businesses, 70–71
Incoming links, in Web sites, 131–132
Information:
    eBay and power of, 66–67
    using the Internet for, 77
Information products:
    benefits of, 89–90
    creating winning, 94–95
    delivery of, 89
    determining demand of, 88–89
    sale of, 36, 67
    selling online, 91–92
    selling other people's products, 93–94
    types of, 87–88, 91
Interests, 7–8
Internet. *See also* Web sites
    affiliate sales sites on, 33–34
    auction sites on, 33
    business success and, 143
    creating presence in, 17–18
    education sites on, 37–38
    entertainment sites on, 31–33
    gambling and adult sites on, 46–48
    membership sites on, 40
    social networking sites/forums on, 34–37
Internet-based news readers, 31
Internet business, 6. *See also* Online business
    desires and, 8–10
    equipment for, 105
    interests, talents, or expertise and, 7–8
    publicity for success of, 141–145
Internet income streams, 65–68
Internet marketers:
    delegation and, 198–199
    legal issues of, 202–204
    mastermind groups for, 195–197

Internet marketing, 6, 77, 145–147, 195–197
Introductory phase, of products, 55

J

Joint ventures (JVs), 134–139

K

Keyword search, 88–89
Knox, Tim, 90–95

L

"Legal Issues for Internet Marketers" (Silber), 202–204
Leung, Simon, 149, 150–152
Linear giving/growth, 44
Links, incoming, 131–132
Long Run Marketing, 85, 86

M

Mac news readers, 31
"Made You Look!" (Friesen), 152–155
"Make Sure Your Customers Actually Get the Benefits" (Harris), 188–193
Marketing, multilevel/network, 40–42. *See also* Internet marketing; Online business marketing
Mastermind group, power of, 194–197
"Mastermind Groups for Internet Marketers" (Hibbler), 195–197
Membership sites, 40
Merchandise. *See* Physical products
Merchant partners, selecting, 72–77
Merchant's program, qualification for, 76
Message boards, 137
MLM. *See* Multilevel marketing (MLM)
Mograbi, Mike, 208–216
Money, affiliates and making, 71–72
Multilevel marketing (MLM), 40–42
MySpace site, 35, 81–82, 84, 146

N

Networking, 137
Network marketing, 40–42
The New American Land Rush: How to Buy Real Estate with Government Money, 34, 37
"A New Model of Social Networking" (Heyer), 83–86
News:
    blogs, 28–29
    popular readers, 31
    sites, 26–28

Newsgroups, 137, 140
Newsletters, 140
News You Can Use (Vitale), 140

O

Oden, Nerisssa, 95–101
Offer(s):
    in e-mail, 128
    in sales letters, 121
    to unsubscribers, Web site traffic and, 149
Off-line business:
    moving to online, 17–20
    starting, 24
Online auction, as real business, 63
Online auction sites, 33. *See also* eBay
    buying for resale on, 58–59
    promoting, 60
    shipping method, 60–61
    timing your auction, 61
Online business. *See also* Internet business;
        Online business marketing
    finding web hosting company, 110–111
    moving from off-line to, 17–20
    publicity and success of, 107–110
    quality and, 185–193
    setting up infrastructure for, 111–114
    starting, 24–25
Online business marketing. *See also* Internet
        marketing
    affiliate program and, 139–140
    articles and, 128–129
    blogs and, 132–133
    branding and, 134
    e-mail and, 127–128
    of information products, 91
    joint ventures and, 134–139
    multilevel/network and, 40–42
    newsletters and newsgroups and, 140
    press releases/public relations and, 140–141
    search engine optimization and, 129–132
    through social networking sites, 80–86
Online forums, 34
Online search system, 21–22
The other Secrets: Beyond the Law of Attraction
        (Wheeler), 37

P

Package, in sales letters, 122
Partnering, informational products and, 93
Pauley, Penelope J., 11–15
Pauley, Thomas L., 11–15
Payment system, in Web sites, 111
PayPal, 52–53

Pay per click (PPC), Web site traffic and,
        149, 150–152
Pay-per-view streaming video, 99–100
Penalty, in sales letters, 122
Perceived value, selling complex products
        and, 89
Perry, Rhea, 38–40
Personal life:
    business and, 4–5
    current situation of, 5–7
    desires and, 8–10
    ideal day in your, 10–11
    interests, talents, or expertise and, 7–8
    power, gift of, 12
Physical products, sales of, 23–26
Podcasting, 143
Porn sites. *See* Gambling and adult sites
Power, 36, 95
Powersellers, path of, 62–63
PPC. *See* Pay per click (PPC)
Press releases, 140–141
Price/pricing:
    auction items, 56–58
    of products and affiliate programs, 75
    of products in Web sites, 162
    in sales letters, 122
Print media, 142
Products:
    affiliate programs and selecting, 75
    lifecycle of, 55
    in sales letters, 122
"Profitably Naming Your New Internet
        Business" (Yudkin), 107–109
Project file, in video, 98
Promise, in sales letters, 122
Psychological steps, in writing sales letters,
        122–126
Publicity, 82, 153
"Publicity Secrets to Attain Massive Success
        for Your Internet Business" (Jennings),
        141–145
Public relations, 140–141

Q

Quality, building business and, 181–183

R

Radio interviews, 141–142
Real estate business online, 21–23
Rebrandable products, Web site traffic
        and, 148
Rent A Coder site, 118–119, 133, 134

Resources, 56–57, 58
RSS technology, 30–31, 133

S

Sabol, Paulie, 42, 43–46
SAFE Ports Bill, 47
Sales:
    automating, information products and, 92
    of information products, 36–37
    of physical products, 23–26
Sales letters, 121–126
Sales management tools, 64
Schank, Roger, 167, 170
Search engine optimization (SEO):
    content and design and, 131
    incoming links and, 131–132
    page title and, 131
    Web site ranking and, 129–130
Search engines, 26, 60
The Secret (Vitale), 36
Sellers, 58, 64
Selling:
    at auction sites, 60
    complex products, 89
    at eBay, 54–56, 57–58
    e-books, 67–68
    information products, 67–68, 93–95
Sense of overwhelm, Internet presence
    and, 20
SEO. *See* Search engine optimization (SEO)
Server capacity, web hosting companies and,
    110
The 7 Day eBook (Vitale), 90
Shawn Collins' Affiliate Tip blog, 74
Shipping, 60–61, 92
Silber, Bob, 202–204
The Silent Machine Hiding on eBay (Cochrum), 66
Silver level PowerSeller, 62
Single-page sales site, 119–120
Social networking sites/forums, 34–36, 80–86
Social proof concept, in marketing, 83–86
Software:
    affiliate program, 113
    for creating videos, 97
    for creating Web sites, 118
    as information product, 88
    locating free video encoder, 99
    for membership sites, 40
    for online gambling, 46
    for online transfer of cash, 46
    WordPress, 118
Spam, 48, 200–201
Spiridellis, Evan, 31–32
Spiridellis, Gregg, 31–32

Squeeze page, 120
Streaming video files, 99–100
Success:
    affiliate sites and, 71
    of Internet marketer, 141–145
    planning for, 205–216
Support services, for World Wide Web, 26

T

Talents, 7–8
Teleseminars, business success and, 143,
    145–147
Television, business success and, 142
Tell Me a Story (Schank), 167, 170
Testimonials, Web site traffic and, 148
Thinking, positive, 13
This Land (cartoon), 32
"The Three Keys to Success" (Audio), 15
"Three Secrets to Making Sales Letters Sell"
    (Heindricks), 121–126
Timing, auction and, 61
Trademarks, 201–202
Traffic, Web sites, 147–149
Trust, social proof and, 84
TuYu, LLC., 83–86
Two-tier agreement, 76

U

U. S. Patent and Trademark Office (USPTO),
    203
UIGEA. *See* Unlawful Internet Gambling
    Enforcement Act (UIGEA)
Uniform resource locator (URL), 106
Unique selling proposition (USP), 138
Unlawful Internet Gambling Enforcement Act
    (UIGEA), 47
URL. *See* Uniform resource locator (URL)
"Use MySpace to Build Your eBay Business"
    (Ginsberg), 81–82
USP. *See* Unique selling proposition (USP)
USPTO. *See* U. S. Patent and Trademark
    Office (USPTO)

V

Videos:
    creating with software, 96–99
    hosting, 100
    of information products, 88
    making, 98
    pay-per-view streaming video, 99–100
    video DVD disc, 98–99

Videos: (*continued*)
  video file download, 99
  Web site traffic and, 147
Viral products, Web site traffic and, 148
Visibility, 17–18, 89
Visitors name, collecting, 117
Vitale, Joe:
  hypnotic selling, 171–176
  hypnotic writing products, 34
  information products, 36

W

Warren, Neil Clark, 34–35
Web hosting, 26, 110–111
Webinars, 145–147
"Webiners-The Future of Online Marketing"
    (Edwards), 145–147
Web sites. *See also* Web sites content; Web
    sites infrastructure
  design and physical construction of,
    114–119, 131
  for finding deals online, 21
  increasing traffic of, 147–149
  naming and finding web host, 107–111
  news and general information in, 26–28
  for periodic bargains, 59
  ranking of, 129–130
  statistics of visitors, 144
  universal resource locator, 106
  using hypnotic writing in, 159–166
Web sites content, 117
  creating hypnotic stories, 168–169
  design and, 131
  expanding the updated formula, 163–166
  formula for causing action, 159–162
  four step strategy for, 160–162
  length of, 166–167
  updated formula, 162–163

using hypnotic writing for, 158–159
  using stories for, 167–168, 170–171
Web sites infrastructure:
  affiliate program in, 113–114
  autoresponders in, 112–113
  payment system in, 111
"What's The Best Product to Sell Online?"
    (Knox), 90–95
Wheeler, Jillian:
  getting into Internet marketing, 6
  information products, 34, 37
  Web sites of, 37, 38
"WHOA" formula, in writing sales letters,
    121–122
Windows news readers, 31
WordPress, 110, 118, 133
World Trade Organization (WTO), 46, 47
World Wide Web, 26, 47–48
Writing, hypnotic, 34, 158–181
Writing sales letters:
  five P's of, 122
  psychological steps of, 122–126
  "WHOA" formula, 121–122
Written reports, as information products, 88
WTO. *See* World Trade Organization
    (WTO)

Y

Yahoo!, 25, 129
Your Internet Cash Machine site, 40, 89, 126,
    129, 207
YouTube site, 84, 147
Yudkin, Marcia, 106, 107–110

Z

Zero Limits (Vitale), 36